ARE YC
KILLING YOU?

A Complete Personal Handbook
Of Safety Suggestions
to Incorporate into Your Everyday Life:
Because the Best Defense Is a Good Offensive Plan!

KIMBERLY CHERYL

Outskirts Press, Inc.
Denver, Colorado

Are Your Habits Killing You?
A Complete Personal Handbook Of Safety Suggestions to Incorporate into Your Everyday Life: Because the Best Defense Is a Good Offensive Plan!

Outskirts Press, Inc.
http://www.outskirtspress.com

ISBN: 978-1-4327-1461-1

Outskirts Press and the "OP" logo are trademarks belonging to Outskirts Press, Inc.

PRINTED IN THE UNITED STATES OF AMERICA

DEDICATIONS

With great pleasure I want to thank all the people who have meant so much to me over the years, and who in their own way have helped motivate me to write *Are your Habits Killing You?*

It would be impossible to begin anywhere else than with my family. My husband, Larry, who has taught me about Personal Safety since the first time he jumped out at me from behind a dumpster near our college apartment to show me how quickly and easily a person could be hurt without paying attention. He has also been my greatest supporter in all aspects of my life. I thank him for the countless, sleepless hours he put in editing my writing. His contributions to this book are woven into each and every page.

My parents, grandparents and in-laws showed me how much parents can care for their children. Their love, respect, and support over the years have been constant, a strength that would help any child reach for and achieve their dreams.

My two children are the main reason that I faced this difficult topic head-on. May they have the opportunity to live within a safer community and grow up to achieve all of their goals. My children have shown an incredible depth of loving support and understanding so others can stay safe in our dangerous world; it has given me the strength during the many long hours and late nights that have been necessary to accomplish my missions in life.

To my sisters, Kelly and Kara and my sister-in-law Cindy; my cousin, Tracy and my dearest friends, Kim, Debi, Traci, Kelly for their support through my changing moods and various pursuits. Without them, life would never be the same and all are gifts from above in their own unique way.

In addition, I would like to genuinely thank Paul and Rebecca Schmitz for their partnership in our corporation and their dedication to making Executive Defense a success. Paul is an incredible asset, a knowledgeable educator and a speaker who is appreciated by those he encounters in the "field".

Last but not least, my sincerest respect and gratitude to all those in law enforcement and to those who work endlessly for little monetary reimbursement to help the victims of crime and domestic violence. The endless hours they dedicate to the safety and well-being of others is never fully appreciated. A Special Thank You to Our School's SRO, Officer Doherty. She is not only influential by way of the positive attitudes and behaviors that she helps instill in students, but by the sincere appreciation and respect for law enforcement which she nurtured and encouraged in my daughter and many others through sponsorship of the Police Teen Academy.

CONTENTS

FOREWORD

If there were ever a need to protect ourselves and our families, that need couldn't be greater than it is today. With each passing day, media reports of burglary, car thefts, violence, murders, school shootings, missing, abducted and molested children have placed this issue on the national agenda.

Compounding the problem are the shrinking budgets for law enforcement and the increasing challenges they face to keep drugs and criminals off of our streets. Personal Safety Tips are not propriety information and there are many good books out there that address the subject. You don't have to reinvent safety – you can learn from law enforcement and industry leaders but none of it means anything if you don't put what you've learned into practice!

Personal safety education is something we learn through repetition and reinforcement. *It should be a habit – a natural response to a given situation*. We should not take a class for one day, get excited about safety, and then forget the training and safety information returning to our old possibly dangerous habits. Proper safety education shouldn't be fear inducing. It requires a well thought-out supportive framework that allows us to be educated in a non-threatening, proactive fashion. We need to be "enlightened, not frightened". We need to have the ability to act logically, rather than be paralyzed by fear in a dangerous situation. My husband has always advised me that I need to live in a "Yellow Mode" – not oblivious, not fearful. One needs to be AWARE of their surroundings and should always trust their instincts. That "little voice" is there for a reason – people should heed those "feelings" and not worry about being "rude" – there are polite ways to get out of most situations and if there isn't "it's better to be safe than sorry".

I know there is a lot of information in this book – I did that on purpose. As a busy working mother, I wanted a resource book that I could refer to with information on a variety of issues. My hope is that you will take at least a few of these safety tips and make them a regular part of your life. Some are better than none – work, build and grow your knowledge from there. My other true aspiration in writing this book is to permit you to sleep more comfortably with the confidence and assurance that you have the tools to help yourself and your family avoid and respond to any threat that you might face. BE SAFE!

PREFACE

Life has its' ups and downs. After years of ups, we were due for a down. My husband and I had been blessed with two beautiful children, two full-time jobs that afforded us a fairly comfortable life – him a Probation and Parole Officer, me a Pharmaceutical Representative. In 2007, the circumstances of our life changed dramatically. A part of our life collapsed. My husband's health gave way and I was released from my position after an auto accident left me in need of surgery. A mother's instinct to protect her family came charging to the surface. I needed to find work. I know it may sound dramatic but without employment, and our health situations, we were well on our way to losing everything we worked so hard to build. Our debt began to increase exponentially; we had no health insurance and feared we could end up "on the street". As with all devastating experiences, if you look carefully, there is a silver lining. We decided to combine my desire to help others with my husband's knowledge of safety, self defense, and the criminal mind to create a company that could help others.

I can still remember one of my first years in the field as a pharmaceutical representative. I was working a luncheon program at an inner city hospital. My car was packed with drug samples, my hands were full of food for the office staff waiting inside and my back was to the public. I was engrossed in my thoughts of the upcoming sales meeting and what I needed to say and do to obtain the business. I turned to close my trunk and found myself face-to-face with a pistol. A drug addict wanted what I had in my trunk not knowing it was only Tagamet (for reflux) and antibiotics. I threw my salad at him and ran inside the building. He only took my samples but I will never forget the fear of that encounter and how suddenly it happened.

Now, years later, through my husband's 18 years of training and experience in law enforcement, why not help others avoid similar situations? Through this desire a seed sprouted. *Executive Defense Technology* was born. My dream is becoming a greater reality than I had ever hoped. We have already reached many through our Corporate Training Program and are developing a children's training program. We are growing rapidly and are working closely with the local YMCA and County Police Departments. Together we developed a program entitled *"College Knowledge- Everything You Need To Know Before Leaving Home"* for our young adults – it's held in August before they head off to school. One day, I hope this can be a National Program from which many more can benefit.

Today, there is so much information online it is hard to distinguish truth from fiction. With the addition of the internet into our busy lives, it is easy to gather information but there are many myths and misconceptions circulating relative to personal safety. While they can instill a greater awareness in crime prevention, it is also usually one of these presented strategies which "sounds great" at first glance to the average person that could potentially do more harm than good. Then there are the popular TV shows like CSI and Law and Order, which are two of my family's favorites. The problem with these shows is the portrayal of a "Hollywood" version of Cops and Robbers. They are not necessarily a true reflection of law enforcement and how our criminal system works.

For these and other reasons, I have tried to produce a comprehensive book with helpful guidelines for all – no matter your stage in life. The crime prevention techniques cited in this book were obtained from various outside sources, including, but not limited to, federal, state and local law enforcement officials and crime prevention experts. I believe the information to be accurate and reliable. Yet, I would caution that it cannot be assumed that every possible and acceptable crime prevention procedure is contained in this book. Obviously, abnormal, unusual or individual circumstances may require further or additional information or procedures.

We cannot prevent every crime from occurring, just like a bullet proof vest cannot always completely protect the wearer but, knowledge, awareness, self-defense and carrying non-lethal deterrents are an excellent beginning. I am so thankful that you are taking the time to help keep yourself and your family safe. Together, we can help create a more secure and safer community for all.

GENERAL STATIJTICJ AND THE CRIMINAL MINDJET

The 2005 criminal victimization report by the US Department of Justice – Bureau of Justice Statistics stated that 18 million property crimes (burglaries, motor vehicle thefts and household thefts); 5.2 million violent crimes (rapes/ sexual assaults, robberies, aggravated assaults and simple assaults); and 227,000 personal thefts (picked pockets and snatched purses) were reported to authorities in America.

Violent Crimes in General

- 90% of violent attacks happen in Key-Related situations
- 82% of society will be the victims of a violent crime during their lifetimes
- An average of 80 million crimes of violence are reported each year
- Over 16,000 murders occur on average each year
- 3 out of 4 women will be victims of at least one violent crime during their lifetime

Rape / Sexual Assault

- Every hour 16 women confront rapists
- A woman is raped every 4.5 minutes
- 42% of rape victims tell no one
- Only 5% of all sexual assaults are reported to law enforcement
- 58% of sexual assaults are not reported by the victims to either law enforcement or crisis centers
- 78% of sexual assaults are committed by someone the victim knows
- 42% of sexual assaults occur inside the victim's home
- 3 out of 7 women who are sexually assaulted, are assaulted by multiple assailants
- 22% of sexual predators assault an average of 7 victims before they are caught and convicted
- Only 2% of all sexual assaults result in the assailant (s) being convicted and imprisoned
- The United States has a rape rate 13 times higher than Great Britain (UK), nearly 4 times higher than Germany, and more than 20 times higher than Japan

Violent Assault and Battering

- A woman is beaten by her spouse every 9 seconds
- 3 to 4 million women are battered each year
- More than 1 million women seek medical assistance for injuries caused by battering each year
- Females are approximately 75% of the victims of intimate murders and about 85% of the victims of non-lethal intimate violence
- Women age 16 to 24 experience the highest per capita rate of intimate violence

As common as they are disturbing, sexual assaults against women are on the rise. Sexual assaults remain the most under-reported cases in the criminal justice system. (Statistics compiled by the U.S. Department of Criminal Justice, Senate Judiciary committee reports and the FBI)

Murders in the United States jumped 4.8 % in 2006, and overall violent crime was up 2.5 % for the year, marking the largest annual increase in crime in the United States since 1991, according to figures released by the FBI.

According to a 2006 study released by the Justice Department's Bureau of Justice Statistics, 56% of the violent felons convicted in the nation's 75 most populous counties from 1990 to 2002 had a prior conviction record, 38 % had a prior felony and 15 % had been previously convicted for a violent felony. 36% of the violent felons had at least one active criminal justice status at the time of their arrest. This included 18 % on probation, 12 % on release pending disposition of a prior case and 7% on parole. Nearly 80% of convicted rapists who were released from prison will commit seven more rapes before being arrested again. In 2006, 600,000 parolees were released back into our communities.

Unfortunately, these were the people my husband dealt with on a daily basis for 18 years hoping for those rare "success cases" of a life "turned around". During that time period, he felt a lot of resources were being utilized for the criminals but not much was available to help the victims of crime. That is yet another reason why we started *Executive Defense Technology, LLC* and why he encouraged me to write this book. We have tried to take some of what he learned about criminal behavior and "turn it around". If we could help people understand and "think like the criminal", maybe we could help some of those people avoid becoming victims in the first place. We should keep in mind that nobody is totally immune from people who are highly motivated to do harm but, by being aware of our surroundings, using caution and utilizing simple safety and self-defense techniques, we may discourage them. At the very least, our behavior may cause them to pass us by as a victim or, if we are prepared for an attack, we can lessen the severity of an assault and any potential harm to us.

In addition to violent attacks, in 2005, there were an estimated 18 million property crimes (burglary, motor vehicle thefts and household thefts) and 227,000 personal thefts (picked pockets and snatched purses). (U.S. Department of Justice)

Most of us are law-abiding citizens who choose socially acceptable means to obtain what we want or need. Some people, however, prefer to break the law and use violence, threat of violence, coercion and deception to get what they want. Unfortunately, criminals are not rare in our society. We are at risk at any time and anywhere. So, what makes these individuals "tick"?

The following are just a few of the valuable points that you need to know about the psychological make up of criminals and violent people:

- Extreme egomania/selfishness/me-based orientation
- Poor impulse control
- Manipulative behavior
- Inability to accurately "read" other people's emotions
- Little or no ability to delay gratification
- Disassociation from the negative effects of their actions/guilt
- Your "value" is defined by what you can do for them
- The only constant in their behavior is what benefits/pleases them.

You cannot change these elements in their personality and without outside, long-term professional help/counseling, they will not change their behaviors on their own. No matter how much they say they will. Believe it or not, you already know what the criminal is and what motivates him, you see it all the time in minor forms. What to most people is a minor character flaw is to criminals a major defining element of their personalities.

Each day of your life, you encounter attitudes, behaviors and ways of thinking that are annoying and selfish. Usually, however, these obnoxious people have a form of checks and balances that keep them somewhat in line with societal norms. We tend to automatically assume these checks and balances are always in place. This is the "social contract" that allows people to function and get along together in their day-to-day activities. We don't realize how ingrained and unconscious these rules of behavior and ways of thinking are in us. It is both shocking and unnerving when we encounter those who don't follow or abide by the unstated rules.

What few people realize is that those checks and balances are missing within the criminal or violent person. With the absence of counterbalancing, certain behaviors flourish and grow. What is apparent, to a small degree, in a normal person can be enormous in the criminal. The magnitude and extremes to which criminals are willing to go are unbelievable to most people, something they simply cannot truly comprehend.

Crime and violence are processes that take time to develop. The attack is not the first step. Criminals plan what they are going to do to their victims and will take many steps to ensure that they are successful. Initially, the criminal (or violent person) decides whether or not he can get away with the planned event, "Can I get away with it?" is a major motivator for what people decide to do – or not do.

There is a concept called the triangle among firefighters. Along each side is an element that a fire needs in order to burn. If you take away one of these elements, then the triangle collapses and the fire goes out. Crime is similar: in order for crime to occur, there must be three basic elements

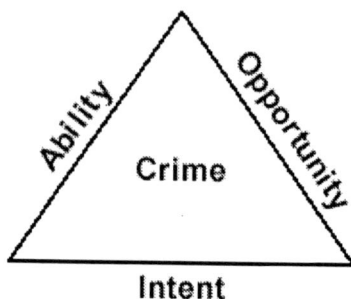

Take away any one of these elements and the triangle collapses. In other words, the crime does not have what it needs to occur. (State of Missouri Training Guide for Probation / Parole Officers)

No one wants to be a victim of violent crime. The key to guaranteeing one's safety is to avoid being selected as a target in the first place. Criminals may use different methods to select their targets but there are common characteristics of this process that determine who ultimately becomes the target. Criminals will attack the person that seems unaware or break into the house that appears vulnerable.

Many times, the criminal will approach you under the guise of normalcy, i.e., needing information or small item (e.g. cigarette). This is a distraction. While he is talking, he is not only getting in position to attack, but a) checking your awareness about what he is doing and b) your commitment to defending yourself.

This is one reason you should always be careful when someone approaches you in a "fringe area" – the area just on the outskirts of a large crowd, an area that would be easy to get you away without being noticed or suspected. A fringe area is where you are close to people, but out of range of immediate help. You won't be mugged in the mall, but will be in the parking lot or bathrooms. ATMs, parking lots, stairwells, public bathrooms and sidewalks should always be considered potential danger areas. Even a separate room in a crowded house can constitute a fringe area, as many women who were raped at parties can attest. Being alone with someone in a fringe area is a major part of the predator's "opportunity". When approached and questioned by a stranger – especially one who makes you uncomfortable, your answer should always be "no" and insist that they keep their distance. Both muggers and stranger rapists often use those techniques.

Then there are times when a person or people will test your boundaries by using escalating outrageous behavior. Every time he is not slapped down (i.e., he is successful), his behavior becomes more and more extreme until finally he attacks. That is a very common interview for date rapists. It is also common when you walk into the middle of a group of loitering thugs, what "supposedly" begins as "just messing with you" can quickly escalate into a robbery or assault – sometimes both.

There are instances when a criminal will put himself in a position to observe you. He may never speak until the attack, but he has been watching all along. He may position himself out of sight in a parking structure and follow you. Sometimes, as in the case of being stalked or with a serial rapist, the predator will watch a victim for days, weeks, or longer before moving to attack.

A criminal does not want to fight you; he wants to overwhelm you. He wants to do it quickly and effectively. If at this point, the assailant decides that he cannot successfully, or easily, attack you he will generally seek easier prey. In the case of an emotionally upset individual, he will change tactics. For example instead of physically assaulting you he may proceed to stand back and verbally abuse you. This allows him to 'win' without putting himself at physical risk.

Subsequently, once he is sure of his ability to succeed and has put you in a position where he can quickly overwhelm you, he will attack. When he attacks, one of the most common methods used by criminals is to try to trap you between himself and a large object, such as a car or a wall. This way he has put himself between you and easy egress. In some instances, the criminal isn't working alone; therefore, you need to be cautious of the fact that this person may have a partner.

In any circumstance, until the criminal is completely out of your sight, you are at risk of his reaction to the crime he has committed, even if you have totally cooperated. The unpredictability of the criminal's reaction is another reason why it is far easier to avoid violence than it is to try to safely extract yourself from the middle of it.

By using self-defense tactics of awareness and defeating a criminal's opportunity instead of attempting to contest him, you can avoid using violence in all but the most extreme circumstances.

Criminals plan what they are going to do to their victims and will take the necessary steps to ensure their success. Accordingly, you should have a plan in place for how to prevent being attacked or to defend against an attack should one occur.

PART I
Child Security

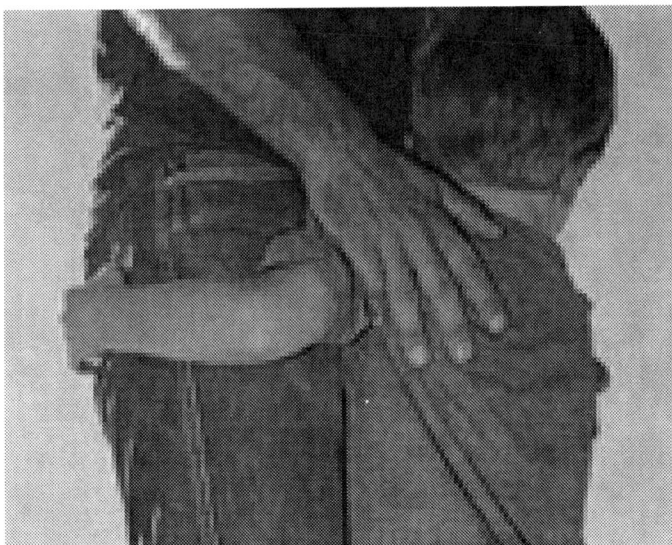

The job of being a parent is one of the most difficult and important jobs anyone can sign up for! (Yet, someone has forgotten to give us each an instruction booklet when we leave the hospital with that new bundle of joy)

Parenting today is a tougher job than it was for the generation before us (just as it was for them compared to previous generations) The challenge is partly due to the stresses and strains of modern life. We have more pressure on us to try and balance work, family and life in general. We just don't have enough hours in the day to do all we need and want to do. It is because our children tend, in ways that we sometimes don't want or expect, to grow up a lot faster than kids did when we were young. And although there are many benign influences in our society, there are a lot of malign ones as well – the dangers of alcohol abuse and drug addiction, earlier sexual maturity and activity, the difficulty when kids start associating with other kids who are leading them astray and so on. *Being a parent is not easy. Being a child is not easy in today's society either!*

Children and teens face difficult choices and we know you want to see them grow up to be productive adults. Whether you have a new baby at home, a young one just starting school, a teen, or a grown college student on campus, it's a different world for children now. Your child has a multitude of safety concerns to deal with that you never faced. Knowing how to help him or her stay safe is a priority for you as a caring parent and adult.

"Child Abducted" …. "School Under Attack"….Crawling across the bottom of our television screens, this message makes the hearts of parents and grandparents across the United States stop. "Do I Know

The Family? The Victim?", "Is it my child's school?", "My grandchild's?" "How many more victims of terrorism will our nation sacrifice?" "How could innocent children be targeted?" When details emerge and the location of the school or missing child become known, a sense of relief rushes in just as quickly. "My child is safe." "I don't have to worry." "It happened over there somewhere." "Such an incident couldn't happen here." "It couldn't happen to my child or in my community." Or could it? The troubling question regarding these incidents is whether something like this could happen to us. And the answer to the question is, "yes, it can happen here." Our schools are not immune to such attacks, and our children are not immune to being abducted. Anyone who thinks otherwise needs a "reality check" regarding the security of our schools and the safety of our children.

Who are the people from whom we have to protect our children? Most times, we don't know them even though we see them every day. Experts tell us they are in our children's environment, but since parents are not trained to recognize them we cannot protect ourselves or our children.

Statistics tell us that as of December 31, 2006, there were 110,484 active missing person records in the NCIC. Juveniles under the age of 18 account for 58,763 (53.18 %) of the records and 12,657 (11.46 %) were for juveniles between the ages of 18 and 20. In addition there are about 115,000 *attempted* abductions of children (those were just the reported cases; thousands more incidents aren't reported). That means that thousands of children have used their "*personal safety skills*" to get away from people who meant to do them harm. The point is we cannot always stop the people who harm children, but we can prepare our children to be among those, who – if they are ever approached or put in harms way – will have the knowledge to keep themselves safe.

2006 NCIC MISSING PERSON ENTRIES

UNDER 18	
	662,228
JUVENILE	
	635,236
ENDANGERED	
	15,379
INVOLUNTARY	
	6,170
DISABILITY	
	3,541
CATASTROPHE	
	107
OTHER	
	1,795
FEMALE	
	377,567
MALE	
	284,655
UNKNOWN	
	6
ASIAN	
	9,880
BLACK	
	200,681
INDIAN	
	9,022
UNKNOWN	
	13,103
WHITE * (including Hispanic)	
	409,542

The people who harm children need to be stopped. This chapter is meant as a handbook against an enemy who has no face, against an enemy who smiles sweetly at us and then commits crimes we cannot imagine. If we lived in a country at war, we would be alert to protecting ourselves and our children. But because the enemy is not a soldier standing with a gun aimed at us, we are lulled into believing there is no one out to harm us. *This suits the perpetrators perfectly.* They would prefer that we believe that violence of any sort won't happen to us. "Maybe the people down the street or on the other side of town, but not us," we desperately want to believe. But the next time you see someone on the news, just look into their faces – the grief, the loss, the fright – they never thought it would happen to them either.

To bury your head in the sand and say my child could not be victimized, in light of all that has happened in this country and continues to happen, is doing your child a disservice. This denial will not change reality. Parents often deny tough subjects because they feel; deep down, that they can't do anything to change the problem. Denial is a form of fear, and fear is removed by KNOWLEDGE.

So why did I write this book? I wrote it for your knowledge, for your safety and the safety of our children. I wrote it for my daughter who we have taught to be open and honest with us. A child we protected from every danger in the world. One who was taught about "stranger danger" and all the risks of the world because of her father's job in law enforcement and the many threats he received. She was probably over protected and knows all about the "evils" of the world. A child who knows self-protection and one who is competent with firearms (she's been an avid hunter and outdoors adventurer since she was four).

I wrote it for this daughter that I admire more than anyone I know. She is a fun-loving, intelligent, caring 13 year old who is also a survivor of "child sexual assault".

Therefore, unfortunately, in writing about keeping our children safe, it is impossible not to cross over into the area of sexual abuse. More than anything, I personally wish that I could turn away from this painful topic. As painful as it is for me as a parent to deal with, I have learned through research that sadly, we (as a family) are not alone. Studies show that one in four girls and one in seven boys under the age of eighteen will experience some form of sexual abuse. Unfortunately, it is the silence about this subject that has allowed sexual abuse to take place generation after generation.

I am hoping that the information in this book will make people get mad, then get serious about learning personal safety. I'm also hoping that no person will ever again have to say, "If I had just…."

Setting the Stage with Proper Education

It's surprising that various child safety programs are on the rise yet child safety is still a huge issue. The reason is simple. Predators will continue to thrive and children will continue to go unprepared simply because many of the programs offered do not address the realities of violent situations.

While safety education is of great importance we know that bad education is worse than no education at all. Simply put, these programs must be modified to reflect the realities of the world we live in so that children can be empowered with real knowledge to keep themselves safe from those who intend to do them harm.

While it's true that "self-defense" is offered in many martial arts schools and even some fitness facilities, we must ask ourselves if it's really self-defense that's being taught. A serious abduction prevention program will not be based on punches, kicks, or fancy martial arts techniques.

These types of skills are next to useless for children whose potential attackers outweigh them by 100 pounds or more. The next thing that qualifies an instructor to offer "reality-based" child abduction prevention classes is the possession of a solid background in both martial arts and various areas of self-defense and security. Being a black belt instructor in one style of martial arts does not automatically qualify anyone to teach child abduction prevention, in fact it may not even qualify them to teach basic self-defense to adults.

There is a difference between martial arts and self-defense. While there may be some similarities in the physical applications between the two, this is generally where the similarities stop. Martial arts self-defense programs, what I refer to as traditional self-defense, generally over-emphasize the physical skills while under-emphasizing or even neglecting the psychological and analytical skills needed to deal with life-threatening situations. The belief is that it's the physical skills that determine the outcome of the altercation when, in fact, it's what the student does *before* the situation turns physical that will determine the ultimate outcome. While physical skills are vitally important, they are the least important of all real self-defense/anti-victimization skills.

So what is Self-Defense?

Self-defense is about staying out of harm's way. It's about learning to detect possible violent situations and dealing with them before they turn violent. Self-defense is **NOT** about letting someone physically assault you so you can, in turn, defend yourself. Once this is understood, self-defense can be approached in a direct and realistic manner.

So, what does real self-defense training consist of? The first step to answering this question involves analyzing violent situations and then reverse-engineering them. In other words, we must take a look at how violent situations occur in the first place so that we can learn how to prevent them from escalating to a physical level. Analyzing the situations in this manner can help us understand that there are so many more things we can do prior to using last-ditch physical skills. In other words, while physical skills are necessary, they should be used last and least.

Let's start from the beginning. How can we prevent potentially violent situations? That's easy, we AVOID such situations. To AVOID situations we must be AWARE of such situations before they happen. So, the first step to dealing with violent situations is using common-sense awareness & avoidance strategies. Ultimately, awareness leads to avoidance and avoidance leads to prevention. Understanding this is the key to real self-defense. If we are aware of potentially violent situations before they happen and we avoid those situations, it's highly unlikely that we would ever have to physically protect ourselves. In short, awareness strategies should form the foundation of any realistic self-defense program that is designed to protect lives. Any program neglecting this foundational area is not based in reality.

What about other necessary skills when awareness & avoidance fails? What about methods of escape? Obviously we don't live in a perfect world. While we may have excellent awareness & avoidance skills there is still a chance that we might find ourselves in a potentially violent situation. Based on this fact, we must have a solid understanding of how and when to escape. A brief search of the internet will bring up the following general statistics regarding child safety…which supports the need for realistic educational safety programs.

- One child is reported missing every 40 seconds
- 2000 children are reported missing every day
- 1 child in 42 will become missing
- Typical molesters will abuse 30 – 60 children before being convicted the first time

- 500,000 children are sexually abused each year
- There is an average of 1 child molester per each square residential mile
- Youth 12 – 17 are 2 to 3 times more likely than adults to be the victims of an assault or rape according to the National Crime Victimization Survey
- In a 2003 survey for the Girl Scouts of the USA, 31 % of girls between the ages of 8 and 12 reported being afraid of becoming kidnapped
- There are more than 100,000 non-family member abductions attempted each year, according to the American Prosecutors Research Institute. Eighty percent of the victims had initial contact with the attacker within a quarter-mile of the victim's home

When then do you start to educate your children?

By the time a child is four, you can start introducing the concept of strangers and tricky people and describe some of the simple tactics they use to lure and harm children. Children require different safety rules and different levels of information depending on their age. As a parent, you have the unique advantage of being able to update their safety knowledge as they mature. You can tailor the information to match your child's distinctive personality, and to fit your child's natural strengths and weaknesses.

Amidst all of the sensationalism about kidnappings, murder, school attacks, very little attention is usually paid to proactive solutions and prevention. No wonder children often feel afraid and helpless. Everyone, even children, feels more confident when they are armed with knowledge and answers to scary questions. If we give children the right knowledge and training, they will generally be able to pull them selves out of a crisis. In fact, experts tell us that with the right knowledge, 85 percent of the dangerous situations children might face can be avoided.

Setting the Stage

It is very important to approach the subject of safety in a non-threatening way. We do not want to make children fearful of potentially dangerous situations or people in general, but we do want to teach them to be cautious and to be able to recognize when something may be wrong. The key is to help children feel empowered and to encourage them to develop and trust their intuition. We want to teach them to be able to talk to you, their caregiver, when something is bothering them. Open communication between parents and children is one of the most important aspects to protecting your child from predators.

It is important to talk openly with your children about all safety issues, including what to do in a potential abduction situation. KNOWLEDGE IS POWER. Talk to your children about the rules pertaining to strangers. Let them know a stranger or predator looks just like any other person and will use any number of ways to lure a child. Remember, the vast majority of children who are victimized know their assailants.

What does the "Bad Guy" look like?

The acclaimed philosopher and expert in emergency response, Pogo, said it all: "We have met the enemy, and he is us."

That's one of the toughest questions to answer and there is no "right answer". The one true fact: we cannot pick them out from the people who live and work within our everyday lives. Child molesters and abductors come in all shapes, sizes, races, sexes, and ages and are motivated by a wide variety of motives. Most are not the typical "dirty old man". That's what makes them so dangerous. Like my daughter's assailant, they can be well educated – doctors, lawyers, teachers – family members who work hard to be viewed as "normal". They are the people that "no one suspected" – never in my wildest dreams did I suspect the events going on with my daughter. Even as I research and study the similar characteristics that molesters DO share, I still do not see my relative fitting into one "category" as a potential molester to be wary of. Maybe as family members we are "too close" to the situation and truly do sink our heads in the sand ignoring the signs that may have been apparent to an objective observer. I'm not sure but, I do know that like most child abductors and molesters, he did have two distinct sides to his personality. He was in effect, a modern-day Jekyll and Hyde and he worked very hard at each role.

Other general characteristics of these predators include but are not limited to:

- They often lack social competence with adults
- They usually seek legitimate access to children through jobs and volunteer work
- They spend unusual amounts of time with children
- They usually seduce children with attention, affection, and gifts
- They, in many cases (but not all), were abused as children. Because they were abused and most likely didn't receive treatment, they rarely acknowledge the hurt they inflict on children.
- Normally, they are not correctable; many studies have shown that people who are attracted to children cannot be changed. It is important to remember that if you know someone who was convicted of child molestation you should not be

lulled into thinking they won't do it again.

- Another important fact is that many abductors and molesters are actually seeking love and affection, but in a distorted way. Most molesters spend days, months or even years "grooming" a child for abuse. Clearly, the abuser is often far from a stranger by the time the actual abuse takes place. It's like a spider spinning a web. They know which children won't put up much resistance and which ones won't tell.

The idea here is to identify inappropriate behavior, and remove the prey (your child) from a possible predator. You should not attack the predator. Be very careful. This knowledge is not meant for use in challenging someone, it is meant to help avoid problems. Be extremely careful not to make accusations. If you suspect something, you shouldn't be afraid to report it to law enforcement, social services or other professionals trained to deal with these problems. We must remember that the majority of people in the world do not abuse or harm children. It will not do us or our children any good to distort the natural and harmless affectionate interactions between children and adults. We simply need the knowledge and the awareness to spot truly inappropriate behaviors and actions.

Here are a few points you can use as guidelines to observe adult's behavior around your children:

- Find out why an adult wants to spend unsupervised time with your child
- Find out what attraction there is for your child to spend a lot of time at an adult's home
- Be watchful of adults who shower your child with gifts or invite them out on outings excessively
- Be wary of adults who use games that are really lures and tricks that will become a means to entrap a

child into a physical relationship.

- No one does something for nothing: if they look too good to be true, they just might be
- Ask for several references, including job and volunteer work, from adults in positions of authority, such as scout troop leaders, and follow up with phone calls to the references.
- Make sure your child knows that he or she should tell you if any adult touches him / her in any way that doesn't feel right (even if it's a trusted teacher, church leader or family member – reassure them that they will not be in trouble and they are doing the right thing – ALWAYS believe your child when they find the courage to tell you)

Since most children are naturally friendly, they must clearly understand these important guidelines:

- A stranger is any person they do not know, including persons they may see regularly, such as a store clerk or a neighbor.
- A person's looks DO NOT matter
- Children must pay attention to an adult's behavior, and recognize when that behavior is wrong or inappropriate

One rule about strangers that we had in our house was "It is okay to talk to strangers that are your size". That way we were able to teach our children the accurate concept of stranger danger, we did not scare them and they were able to socialize in a healthy manor with other children their age.

Children also need to know that touching for the sake of teasing, playing, or affection is always a choice. They must be allowed to set the limits on physical affection and touching such as being kissed, hugged, or tickled. We must not force them to kiss grandpa or let Uncle So and So tickle them if it makes the child uncomfortable. Help your child understand that their safety and comfort is more important than someone else's hurt feelings. Reassure your child that you will deal with the consequences if the adult gets mad.

Tell your child that their body is theirs. Children have the right to say who touches them and how. Children also need to be taught the difference between "good touch" and "bad touch". The easiest way to help children understand this concept is to explain to them that the areas covered by their swim suits are special. It is not okay for someone older to touch or ask to touch these private parts. You should also discuss with your child the natural situations when an adult may have to touch his or her private parts (ie, parent's helping them clean themselves, medical reasons, etc)

When they don't like the way they are being touched, your child should be able to say "NO", along with phrases like "I don't like that", "Don't touch me like that", or "Leave me alone". The child can be instructed to add emphasis to their words with body language such as moving away from the person. Again, your child should know that people who don't respect their wishes not to touch their body are breaking the safety rules. If your child gets in a particularly difficult situation they can say, "Stop or I'll tell." Then your child should definitely tell you or someone they trust. Make sure your child knows that even if they have been threatened by an abuser, these threats are usually hollow. They need to understand that you will always love them, and that they have to tell you about disturbing situations no matter what or how embarrassing they may feel it is. Unfortunately, even if they get the person to stop bothering them, they must inform you because the abuser will seek another victim. If your child tells, then there is a chance that the abuser will be caught and stopped.

Hidden Signs Of Child Abuse

- Your child tells stories of a sexual nature or reports sexual activity.
- Your child has a sudden fear of strangers, a relative or babysitter.
- Your child suddenly becomes unruly and destructive, or shy and withdrawn.
- Your child exhibits a change in behavior at home, school or with friends.
- Your child exhibits a loss of appetite, sleep disturbances, nightmares or bedwetting.
- Your child speaks of pain or itching, or you observe any swelling, bruising or bleeding.

Please note that these signs are only indications of possible abuse but things of which you should definitely take note. Again, always believe what your child is telling you and follow up in an appropriate, calm, discreet manner.

Being Aware and Keeping a Safe Distance

Just like adults, children need to be taught what to do if approached, followed, grabbed or attacked. Most importantly, they need to know how NOT to be a victim. It is then imperative that we incorporate repetition. The more both you and your children practice safety and self-defense skills the more confident you will become. Additionally, as with anything else, repetition allows the skills to be used instinctively when they are most needed.

Children are small, they are weaker than their attackers, and they are vulnerable. However, like women, when armed with the appropriate tools they are not defenseless. The more children practice techniques and talk with their parents about what to do in any given, "scary", situation, the better equipped they will be to react quickly. When in danger, there is no time to "think about what to do". We want our children to be able to respond immediately and know where to go for help afterwards.

Almost every day, child abductions occur or are attempted. They occur in front of homes, schools, shopping malls and on almost any given street where an innocent child walks. Being aware of your surroundings is your best defense!

Whether it's walking to a friend's house or home from the bus stop after school, it is always important to know who is walking or lurking within your immediate vicinity and where a safe place is available for help at a moment's notice. You need to be PREPARED not scared. While walking, always keep your head held high. Look around now and then, always being aware of who is in your immediate area. Standing up straight and walking with confidence makes you look strong and not like a potential target. Continuously scanning your environment is the first step to self-defense. *This is true for adults too!*

Always walk in an open area where you can be seen. Walking through alleys, down dark streets or close to parked cars is the worst place to be. These areas make you vulnerable and an easy target!

24 Safety Tips Every Child Should Know:

- Stay at least an arm's reach *plus* away from people you do not know, even if you have to back up to do it
- Trust your gut feelings (instincts) – if something feels wrong, it probably is!
- Anticipate a dangerous situation. Always be prepared to escape, mentally and physically.
- NEVER open a door to a stranger when home

alone. Do not tell someone on the phone that you are home along. Never give out information on your home and family.

- Know your full name, phone number, address and emergency contacts.
- Walk with confidence – attackers usually select their victims based on body language. Don't look like a victim.
- Be AWARE! Know your environment.
- If you feel threatened by a stranger, don't try to fight, but escape. Run as fast as you can in the opposite direction. Try to find an adult you know or trust. Run towards people, lights and noise.
- Never run towards a car that is in your path. If there is nowhere to run forward, then cross the street and run in the opposite direction.
- If you are followed on foot, turn and point to the person and yell "STRANGER"! Then run as fast as you can to a safe place or person.
- Don't hesitate, React quickly and remember anything you have on you – even a pencil can be used as a weapon.
- If you are lost in a mall or crowded area, don't go to a security guard. It is too easy to impersonate these people. Go to a female clerk with a badge in a store or a mother with young children and ask them to help you. Never search for your parents or guardians on your own, and never go with anyone who is trying to reunite you with them.
- Be careful when you play. Stay away from pools, canals, and other bodies of water unless you are with a trusted adult.
- If someone unfamiliar approaches and invades your "safety zone", you should back up three steps
- Yell from the gut – yell as hard as you can; yell as

loud as you can; yell to attract someone to help you; yell to scare off the perpetrator; yell while you are running to a safe environment

- Make a verbal commotion if someone tries to grab you – yell "FIRE", " This is not my mom / dad", "I'm being kidnapped" (If the person tells you to be quiet, to come along and they won't be hurt, that person is lying)
- DO NOT get into any car unless your parents personally tell you to. Also stay away from anyone who follows you on foot or in a car. You do not need and should not go near a car to talk to the people inside.
- Adults and other people who need help should not be asking a child; they should be asking another adult.
- You should use the "Buddy System" and never go places alone. Always ask your parents' permission to leave the yard or play area or to go over to someone's house. Always ask permission before you go into someone's house. Never go to a public restroom, mall, movie, video arcade or park alone. Take a friend – it's more fun.
- Never, Never Hitchhike
- Don't wear clothes or carry items with your name on the outside, and don't be confused just because a person you don't know calls out your name.
- Be careful playing or riding your bicycle as it gets dark. Sometimes it is difficult for people driving to see you. Wear reflectors and protective clothing if your parents or guardians say you may play outside after dark. Always wear protective head gear.
- People should never ask you to keep a special secret. If they do, tell your parents or a teacher. If someone says they want to take your picture, tell

them "NO" and again, tell your parents or teacher.

- I'm not saying you should be disrespectful but you can be assertive and you have the right to say "NO" to someone, including adults and even relatives or friends who try to touch you on the parts of your body (those covered by a swimming suit). The same is true if they try to take you somewhere against your will!

Many parents use a *special code word* that only the child knows to convey a message should someone other than a parent ask a child to accompany them anywhere. Blue Penguin, Fat Cat, Purple Alligator and Boo Beary have been a few of our "family" code words.

In some families, every person has his own code word. In others, like ours, the family chooses just one "family" code. Choose your code word(s) together. Remember, like passwords for your computer, you don't want to use something that would be too easy or obvious to guess like the name of a relative or family pet. Many times, an abductor is not a stranger to the child. Abductors carefully watch children day by day to get a good idea as to the child's routine. At times, abductors are bold enough to mingle with parents who are waiting for their children, listening to all the conversations. Through these many habits, an abductor may accidentally stumble on your family code if it is too apparent.

Therefore, choose words or phrases that are out of the ordinary or are personal to your family, such as names of places you recently visited. Keep your words short, silly and simple so even the youngest member of the family has no problem remembering. Explain to your child why he needs a code word and when he will use it. (ie, tell him that occasionally there may be times when you cannot get to school or sports to pick him up in time. On those days, make sure the person who is there knows the code word).

The family code word is the only thing that a child should listen for when someone other than the planned driver arrives to pick them up. Don't forget to change your code after it has been used.

In addition, you can use code words to:

- Get yourself out of dangerous situations (In our training class, we teach sales people to have code words that everyone in the office knows. That way help can be sent immediately to a person out in the field who requires assistance or feels like they are in a potentially dangerous situation and wants "out".)
- Get others out of dangerous / bothersome situations - **Code names.** If you are bothered by frequent calls from strangers, you might set up a code name to be used by friends and family members. **Example:** A group of teenagers pestered an older woman by pretending to be her grandson Jason. The grandmother notified the phone company to see if they could trace the calls, and then she and her grandson worked out a signal. Jason would ask for "Hank" whenever he called. That way, the grandmother knew it was her grandson and not the other kids. From time to time, they changed the code word to be sure no one could bother the grandmother.
- Keep someone from walking into a dangerous situation (Say there is an intruder in your home late at night and your teenager comes in from a party unsuspectingly. You can very carefully tell the child that you had forgotten your red folder in the car after work and need it. Knowing that is your family code word for danger, the child can quickly turn back around, leave and run to the neighbor's house or use their cell phone to call 9-1-1 and summons

help) And as we just discussed, identify and thwart possible abductors.

Finally, even after practicing all these safety techniques, there are instances that a child may unfortunately still be kidnapped. If that should occur, discuss with them how to escape a kidnapper:

Your Child should not to be afraid to tell you or a trusted adult or teacher if they feel threatened, even if someone has told them not to talk. If victimized it is never their fault and never something they should be ashamed of or something that they hide from their parents or other caregivers. Tell your children you love them and that if they disappear, no matter what their kidnapper says, you will never stop loving them and you will never stop looking for them.

Yell, scream, fight and run from any potential abductor. No matter what their assailant says, make as much noise and attract as much attention as they can.

If on their bike, grip the bike. The kidnapper can't get them and their bike into a car. If on the street and they can't run, grab a street light, traffic sign, trash can, mail box or other fixed object while yelling for help.

If the kidnapper points a gun at them, run any way. Most kidnappers don't want to attract attention by firing a gun. It's better to be wounded and left to get help from others then to go off with a kidnapper who can then have his way with you and in a worst case scenario kill you.

If grabbed, twist your body and scream "this is not my dad (or my mom)!"

If your assailant grabs you by your coat or backpack, twist out of his grip, leaving him with the coat or backpack as you run and scream toward another nearby adult. Attract the attention of this adult by grabbing and holding on to him or her.

If forced into the front seat of a 4-door car or van, immediately jump into the back seat, open the rear door and escape. (Don't put on a seatbelt as this will obviously slow your escape time.)

- Grab the keys from the kidnapper's car and throw them out the window.
- If in traffic, step on the accelerator and make the car crash into the car in front of it. Or poke the driver in the eyes and make him crash
- Honk the horn and try to force the kidnapper to wreck the car.
- Do not eat or drink anything your kidnapper gives to you (it may be drugged).
- If your kidnapper takes you into a store, knock things down, break bottles, yell and scream that you have been kidnapped.
- If you're held in a house, flash the lights on the front porch off and on. If in an upper apartment, flood the bathroom to cause water to flood the apartment below.
- Never stop trying to escape and always take the opportunity to use a phone to call 911 and ask for help.

Discuss and practice these things with your children. While doing everything we can to prevent our children from becoming the victim of a kidnapper, we need also equip them with the above information to help them escape should they be taken by an assailant. Information is vital and can save the life of your child.

Youth Violence

Homicide is the second leading cause of death among young people ages 15 to 19. Among African American youths in that age group, homicide is the leading killer. Within this group, there is an average of 9 youths killed each day due to violence. Just as alarming as the number of young people dying from violence is the number of young people who are committing violent acts. Among the homicide offenders in 2000 whose age was known by authorities, approximately 48% were 24 or younger and 9% were younger than 18.

Violence does not have to be fatal to greatly affect individuals and communities. Violence-related injuries can leave emotional and physical scars that remain with victims long after the violent event has occurred. The rates of nonfatal victimization for rape, sexual assault, robbery, and aggravated assault are higher among people under age 25 than among other age groups. (FBI Uniform Crime Reports. Washington, DC: FBI, 2000)

Bullying

Some parents don't think bullying is a big deal. They think it's a rite of passage to adulthood, that it's just kids being kids. But for kids, bullying is one of the biggest problems they face. In fact, every day 160,000 kids miss school because they're scared of bullying.

A lot of the time kids don't tell their parents that they're being bullied. They may be embarrassed, or they may think that telling will make the bullying worse. To help their children, parents may need to do some detective work to spot the clues that bullying is happening. Here are some signs that a child is being bullied:

- Withdrawal
- Drop in grades
- Torn clothing
- Loss of friends
- Avoidance of school and other activities
- Bruises

- Need for extra money or supplies

A big, tough kid stops a smaller kid on his way to school and threatens to hurt him unless he hands over his homework. The popular girls at school won't let anyone sit at their lunch table except their friends. These two bullying scenarios and others happen more often than most adults realize. 74% of 8 to 11-year-olds say teasing and bullying happen at their school. But what exactly is bullying?

Bullying is:

- fighting, threatening, name calling, teasing, or excluding someone repeatedly and over time
- an imbalance of power, such as size or popularity
- physical, social, AND emotional harm
- when someone is willing to hurt another person to get what he or she wants

The effects of bullying can be severe and long lasting. Bullying doesn't only negatively affect its victims but also the bullies themselves.

Kids who are bullied are more likely to:

- do poorly in school
- have low self-esteem
- be depressed
- turn to violent behavior to protect themselves or get revenge on their bullies

Kids who bully are more likely to:

- do poorly in school
- smoke and drink alcohol
- commit crimes in the future

When Your Child Is Being Bullied

Parents can play a central role to preventing bullying and stopping it when it happens. Here are a few things you can do.

- Teach kids to solve problems without using violence and praise them when they do.
- Give children positive feedback when they behave well to help their build self-esteem. Help give them the self confidence to stand up for what they believe in.
- Ask your children about their day and listen to them talk about school, social events, their classmates, and any problems they have.
- Take bullying seriously. Many kids are embarrassed to be bullied. You may only have one chance to step in and help.
- If you see any bullying stop it right away, even if your child is the one bullying.
- Encourage your child to help others who need it.
- Don't bully your children or bully others in front of them. Many times kids who are bullied at home react by bullying other kids. If your children see you hit, ridicule, or gossip about someone else they are also more likely to do so themselves.

If you think your child is being bullied or if your child has told you that he or she is being bullied, you can help. Parents are often the best resource to build a child's self confidence and to teach him / her how to best solve problems. Here are a few ways you can help:

- Talk to your child's teacher about it instead of confronting the bully's parents. If the teacher doesn't act to stop the bullying, talk to the principal.

- Help your child act with self confidence. With him or her, practice walking upright, looking people in the eye, and speaking clearly.
- Involve your child in activities outside of school. This way he or she can make friends in a different social circle.

When Your Child Is the Bully

It's hard for any parent to believe that their child is a bully, sometimes it happens. But just because your child bullies doesn't mean that he or she will bully forever. Parents are one of the best resources to help their child stop bullying and start interacting positively with their classmates.

Your child may bully if, he or she

- lacks empathy and doesn't sympathize with others
- values aggression
- likes to be in charge
- is an arrogant winner and a sore loser
- fights often with brothers and sisters
- is impulsive

What you can do to stop your child from bullying

- Take it seriously. Don't treat bullying as a passing phase. Even if you're not worried about long lasting effects on your child, another child is being hurt.
- Talk to your child to find out why he or she is bullying. Often, children bully when they feel sad, angry, lonely, or insecure and many times major changes at home or school may bring on these feelings.

- Help build empathy for others and talk to your child about how it feels to be bullied.
- Ask a teacher or a school counselor if your child is facing any problems at school, such as if your child is struggling with a particular subject or has difficulty making friends. Ask them for advice on how you and your child can work through the problem.
- Ask yourself if someone at home is bullying your child. Often, kids who bully are bullied themselves by a parent, family member, or another adult

Male vs Female Bullies

When most people picture a "typical" bully, they imagine a boy who is bigger or older than his classmates, who doesn't do well in school, who fights, and who likes it when others are scared of him. Girls usually face a different type of bully, one who may not look as scary from the outside but who can cause just as much harm.

The typical girl who bullies is popular, well-liked by adults, does well in school, and can even be friends with the girls she bullies. She doesn't get into fist fights, although some girls who bully do. Instead, she spreads rumors, gossips, excludes others, shares secrets, and teases girls about their hair, weight, intelligence, and athletic ability. She usually bullies in a group and others join in or pressure her to bully. This kind of bullying can have just as serious consequences as physical bullying. It can cause a drop in grades, low self esteem, anxiety, depression, drug use, and poor eating habits in girls who are bullied. This kind of bullying is harder to see.

What You Can Do

Parents and other adults can help girls beat bullying by

teaching them how to stand up for themselves and their friends and by taking action themselves. Here are a few things to remember:

- Encourage kids to be kind and to help others, particularly if they see someone being bullied. Praise them when they do so.
- Tell girls they are special, and point out why.
- Help girls get involved in activities outside of school so they can make friends in different social circles.
- Don't push girls to be in the "right" class or on the "right" sports team. Let them choose what to play and with whom.
- Stop bullying when you see it. Don't let anyone, even your daughter, make fun of someone else even if she says she is only "joking."
- Be a good example. Don't gossip or make fun of others in front of young girls.
- Talk to girls about their friends, what they do together, and how they treat each other. Ask them what makes a good friend, and whether their friends have these qualities.
- If you know bullying is happening at school, speak to school officials and ask what they are doing to stop it.

Raising confident and healthy girls is particularly challenging today. Many elementary school girls worry about clothing, popularity, and their weight more than traditional childhood activities. But having mature interests often puts young girls in situations they aren't ready for and that their parents don't expect them to experience until they are older. Girls today face shortened childhoods. They face a lot of pressures, including pressure to dress a certain way, pressure to seem older by trying and using drugs and alcohol, and sexual pressure from classmates, online sources, and the media. Girls can make healthy decisions in even the most difficult situations, but they need to be prepared. Adults can help give girls the confidence to stand up for themselves and do the right thing by starting early and talking about the tough issues girls may face.

Establishing School Safety Guidelines

Our nation's schools should be safe havens for teaching and learning, free of crime and violence. Although there is a large amount of attention devoted to isolated incidents of extreme school violence, what exactly is the state of safety within our educational systems?

In a report published jointly by the National Center for Education Statistics (NCES), Institute of Education Sciences (IES) in the U.S., Department of Education and the Bureau of Justice Statistics (BJS) in the U.S. Department of Justice, the 2004-05 school year had an estimated 54.9 million students enrolled in preK through12th grade. The report findings were as follows:

- From July 1, 2004, through June 30, 2005, there were 21 homicides and 7 suicides of school-age youth (ages 5-18) at school. Combined, this number translates into about 1 homicide / suicide per 2 million students enrolled during 2004/2005 school year.
- In 2004, students ages 12-18 were victims of about 1.4 million non fatal crimes at school, including about 863,000 thefts and 583,000 violent crimes – 107,000 of which were serious violent crimes (rape, sexual assault, robbery and aggravated assault)
- *These figures represent victimization rates of 33 thefts and 22 violent crimes, including 4 serious*

violent crimes, per 1,000 students at school in 2004.

- In 2005, 10 % of male students in grades 9-12 reported being threatened or injured with a weapon on school property in the past year, compared with 6 percent of female students.

- In 2003-04, teachers' reports of being threatened or attacked by students during the previous 12 months varied according to their school level. Secondary school teachers were more likely than elementary school teachers to have been threatened with injury by a student (8 vs 6 %). However, elementary school teachers were more likely than secondary teachers to report having been physically attacked (4 vs 2 %)

- 10 % of central city school teachers, 6% of urban fringe school teachers and 5% of rural teachers were threatened with injury during 2003-04.

- Public school teachers were more likely than private school teachers to have been threatened (7 vs 2 %) or physically attacked (4 vs 2%).

- With regard to other frequently occurring discipline problems in public schools (those occurring at least once a week), 27% reported student bullying (pushed, shoved, tripped or spit on), 11 % reported student verbal abuse to teachers, 3 % reported widespread disorder in classrooms, and 19 % reported student acts of disrespect for teachers. About 17% of public schools reported undesired gang activities and 3% reported undesirable cult or extremist activities.

- In 2005, 43% of students in grades 9-12 consumed at least one drink of alcohol anywhere, and 4 % consumed at least one drink on school property during the previous 30 days;.

- 21% of students in grades 9-12 in 2005 reported

using marijuana anywhere during the past 30 days, and 5% reported using it on school property during that same time period.

Now that we know the statistics and what the risks are in our schools, what do we do about it? First, instead of reacting and responding to a situation of violence and then letting it fade into the background, we must program school protection permanently into our emergency response hard drives. If it's permanent like any other program, confusion and panic won't run rampant in the event of an attack and hopefully, they will be prevented from occurring in the first place. We must strike a balance between preparing for the unthinkable without giving way to unreasonable fear. The odds of a school attack in our community are admittedly low. The odds of any given police officer being shot making a routine traffic stop are also low, yet they train for that eventuality on a regular basis.

Richard Fairburn and Col. David Grossman note in their book ***Preparing for School Attacks*** that the situation of school attacks is very much like fire protection. "The possibility of a student being killed or seriously injured by violence is significantly greater than the probability of being killed or seriously injured by fire. No child has been killed by school fire in North America in over a quarter of a century, but in the 2004/2005 school year, 48 people were murdered in American schools. These are usually random acts of violence, or shootings by students as opposed to acts of terrorism, but the defense against terrorist attacks in our schools is largely the same as the defense against school shootings.

Thus our children are dozens of times more likely to be killed by violence than fire, and thousands of times more likely to be seriously injured by violence as compared to fire. Yet, in any school you can look around and see fire sprinklers, smoke alarms, fire exits, and fire extinguishers. If we can spend all that money and time preparing for fire (and we should, since every life is precious) shouldn't we spend time and money preparing for the thing that is far more likely to kill or injure our child?

The most negligent, unprofessional, obscene words anyone can ever say are: "It will never happen here." When someone asks, "Do you really think there will be a terrorist act or a school shooting here?" Just point to the fire exit and say, "Do you really think there will be a fire here?" No, we don't think there will ever be a fire here. But we would be morally, criminally negligent if we did not prepare for the possibility. And the same is far, far truer of school violence."

So what signs should teachers and school personnel consider questionable behavior? And how should these issues be addressed for a more positive outcome?

Under the intense spotlight of national media coverage, a tragedy such as the Columbine High School or Virginia Tech College shootings spread horror, shock, and fear to every corner of the country. Educators, mental health professionals, legislators, law enforcement officers, parents, students, and the rest of the public all share a sense of frustration and helplessness and a compulsion to take some quick action that can prevent similar incidents in the future. Though understandable, this impulse can lead communities to forget the wisdom of H. L. Mencken's aphorism: "For every problem, there is a solution which is simple, neat, and wrong." In a knee-jerk reaction, communities may resort to inflexible, one-size-fits-all policies on preventing or reacting to violence.

News coverage magnifies a number of widespread but wrong or unverified impressions of school shooters. Among them are:

- School violence is an epidemic.
- All school shooters are alike.

- The school shooter is always a loner.
- School shootings are exclusively revenge motivated.
- Easy access to weapons is THE most significant risk factor.

Unusual or aberrant behaviors, interests, hobbies, etc., are hallmarks of the student who is destined to become violent.

School shootings and other forms of school violence are not just a school's problem or a law enforcement problem. They involve schools, families, and communities. An adolescent comes to school with a collective life experience, both positive and negative, shaped by the environments of family, school, peers, community, and culture. Out of that collective experience come values, prejudices, biases, emotions, and the student's responses to training, stress, and authority. His or her behavior at school is affected by the entire range of experiences and influences. No one factor is decisive. By the same token, however, no one factor is completely without effect, which means that when a student has shown signs of potential violent behavior, schools and other community institutions do have the capacity – and the responsibility – to keep that potential from turning real.

Signs or Symptoms of Potential Problem Behavior

- Infatuation with death or weapons
- Unusual art projects or creative writing
- Unusual reading choices (ie, para-military or occult)
- Satanic or occult clothing, jewelry, etc
- Association with gangs, hate groups, militia groups
- Talk of suicide

- Extreme anger problems
- Overly withdrawn or disassociated – anti-social
- Jokes about any of the above
- Verbal or written threats
- Changes in Normal Behavior Patterns – Recent decline in attendance and performance in school and/ or recent, dramatic change in appearance
- Inappropriate clothing for seasonal conditions (jackets when none are needed, clothing that is overly large to conceal items)
- Numbness or lack of emotional attachment
- Negative self-image and unstable self-esteem
- Guns in the home, proficiency with firearms
- Average to above average IQ
- Covert vandalism and/or dishonesty – distrust of authority
- Immature and socially inadequate, rejected, teased and bullied by peers
- Narcissistic attitude of superiority
- Projects blame
- Sensitive to criticism
- Violent fantasies
- Stalking of Females
- Brags about violence and cruelty

One of these items in and of itself may not be cause for concern but with a few of these behavior patterns together may make you question the student's motives. One example may be a change in a child's demeanor along with a change in dress. This may signal a problem / concern that should be discussed with your co-workers and administration so further action can be taken if needed. Remember though, a great many adolescents who will never commit violent acts will show some of the behaviors or personality traits included on the list!

Unfortunately, there is no profile of a school killer. The killers are white, Native American, African American, and Hispanic. They are upper class, middle class, and lower class. They come from broken families and intact families. While most are male, several are females. Yet, the Secret Service does say that there are usually always indicators that a kid is thinking about killing or committing a violent crime before he / she acts. It is the job of teachers, parents, and police officers to hone in on these indicators. We need to be *cautious* but not overly paranoid so that we go to the complete opposite extreme and ruin a "good kids" life because he is going through a normal phase of rebellion, etc.

Finally, all threats are NOT created equal. However, all threats should be assessed in a timely manner and decisions regarding how they are handled must be done quickly.

In today's climate, some schools tend to adopt a one-size-fits-all approach to any mention of violence. The response to every threat is the same, regardless of its credibility or the likelihood that it will be carried out. In the shock-wave of recent school shootings, this reaction may be understandable, but it is exaggerated – and perhaps dangerous, leading to potential underestimation of serious threats, overreaction to less serious ones, and unfairly punishing or stigmatizing students who are in fact not dangerous. A school that treats all threats as equal falls into the fallacy formulated by Abraham Maslow: "If the only tool you have is a hammer, you tend to see every problem as a nail." Every problem is not a nail, of course, and schools must recognize that every threat does not represent the same danger or require the same level of response.

Some threats can herald a clear and present danger of a tragedy on the scale of Columbine and Virginia Tech. Others represent little or no real threat to anyone's safety. Neither should be ignored, but reacting to both in the same manner is ineffective and self-defeating. In every school, an established threat assessment procedure managed by properly trained staff can help school administrators and other school staff to distinguish between different levels of threats and choose different appropriate responses.

Threat assessment seeks to make an informed judgment on two questions: how credible and serious is the threat itself? And to what extent does the predator appear to have the resources, intent, and motivation to carry out the threat?

Practice, Practice, Practice

Although we can't specifically "profile" the next violent student, law enforcement agencies and school need to have a contingency plan in place for all forms of school violence. Like working with the fire department when your school has a fire drill, you need to work with and coordinate safety plans with your local police department. Every classroom needs to be assessed, just like each classroom needs a separate fire plan. In some rooms, you can secure students in the room, locking and/or barricading doors. Other locations may not be securable (like the Columbine Library) and the drill must be to move to another room that can be secured. The room needs to be an area that can slow down an intruder or shooter long enough for the police to arrive and respond. When the police arrive, the children should be advised to "Lie down and stay down until told otherwise".

Deciding to evacuate may be another viable option in this situation but that is a judgment call. All contingency plans should incorporate the local Fire Department since they already have blue prints of your property. These plans should also utilize the knowledge and experience of the SRO (student resource officer – police presence in our schools deters violence and I can't tell you what an asset our SRO is at my daughter's school! Every Middle and High School needs one if possible).

Experts agree the single most important factor in surviving any type of criminal attack is to have an overall safety strategy before you need it.

Some guidelines that may assist you in preventing violence and/or avoiding direct involvement with violence elsewhere in the school:

- Teachers should be sensitive to the mutterings and whispers of potential confrontation
- Alert the principal, no school personnel should confront a violent situation alone
- If students have lockers in the hallway for storage, do not allow book bags in the classroom
- If practical, leave doors to the hallway open during class (it is possible that, as a situation develops in your classroom, a passing teacher or students can alert someone else in the building to provide assistance
- If you do hear gunfire from anywhere in the building, immediately shut the door and let no student in or out until you are informed that the situation is resolved
- If a student does indicate intent to do harm, such as pointing a weapon or threatening someone, as hard as it is to do, you must remain calm. As frightened as you are, you must realize that you are the person who is most likely to be able to remain calm.
- Do not come between the student with the weapon and the exit
- Approaching a student with a weapon and daring him / her to pull the trigger, makes for interesting Hollywood movies but should never be attempted in the real world no matter how well you know the student. A weapons situation in school is not the time for false bravado

Again, these are just merely guidelines and no two weapons situations are similar. Your best judgment is your greatest ally. Once you, your administration and law enforcement come together to develop your school security preparations and response plans, <u>keep them current</u>. Motivate school personnel to stay sharp and be alert. School attacks, like other violent crimes, tend to ebb and flow in their frequency. Just like awareness while walking in transitional or public areas, being aware of your surroundings all the time at school can prevent someone from being able to use the element of surprise to take advantage of you. Eventually, like the fire drill, it will become a part of your natural routine.

School Bus Stop Safety Issues:

- Parents should insure that if possible, an adult waits with children at school bus stops (not always possible with one parent families or where both parents work), but something could be worked out with all parents of children at the bus stop to be there on a rotating basis.
- Know the path your child takes to and from their home to the school bus stop.
- Avoid short cuts through woods, alleys, parks, or other areas where they could be alone.
- Identify safe houses along the way that your child could run to or into for help if needed.
- Insure your child does not have their name visible on their backpack, etc., as this would enable a potential abductor to call out to the child by name.
- If your child feels concerned for their safety, they should always tell their parents and the bus driver of any such concern.

- If approached on the way to or from the bus stop or at the bus stop, tell your parents, the bus driver, and school officials.
- Report any suspicious vehicle, writing down the license number and providing it to school and law enforcement officials.
- Stand away from any vehicle that stops near the bus stop and do not allow yourself to come close to or enter the vehicle of someone you don't want to.
- Run from anyone displaying a weapon, this while throwing books, yelling, and making as much noise as they can. Under no circumstances go with an abductor. Kick, bite but no matter what the threat, do not go along with your kidnapper. Once he takes you away, your chances of survival greatly diminish.

Make Sure Children Know the Rules of Pedestrian Safety

Although people of all ages are at risk for injury, children are especially vulnerable. Children are particularly at risk when they dart out unexpectedly into traffic, enter a street in the middle of a block or dash into the street from between parked cars. To keep children safe, it's critical that we remember to supervise them as they approach and cross streets, no matter how mature or street savvy they seem to be. It's also important to plan safe walking routes for school-aged children and to regularly review pedestrian safety tips.

Advise children to follow these tips to enable them to see potential hazards:

- Don't cross a roadway in the middle of the block. If

a crosswalk isn't available, stop at the curb or edge of the road and look for approaching vehicles before stepping into the street.

- Always look to the left, to the right and back to the left for approaching traffic. Continue to look until you have crossed the street safely.
- If your view of approaching traffic is blocked by parked cars (or something else), move out to where a driver can see you and you can see an approaching vehicle.
- Watch out for cars backing out of parking spaces or driveways
- Where there are no sidewalks, walk facing traffic and keep as far to the left side of the roadway as possible
- Walk directly across the street; do not walk diagonally.
- Being in a crosswalk doesn't necessarily mean drivers will stop for you. Be Cautious!
- At traffic signals with pedestrian lights, wait until the "walk" signal appears

Outdoor Safety

Each year, about 260 children under 5 drown in swimming pools. In addition, the suction from drains in swimming pools and spas, under certain conditions, can trap swimmers underwater. To help protect your family, be sure to take the following steps:

Use Layers of Protection

To prevent swimming pool drowning, layers of protection are essential. Place barriers completely around the pool, closely supervise young children, and be prepared in case of emergency.

In addition:

- If a child is missing, always look first in the pool. Seconds count!
- Knowing how to swim doesn't make a child drown-proof. Never use flotation devices as a substitute for supervision.
- Keep rescue equipment and a phone next to the pool.
- Learn cardiopulmonary resuscitation (CPR).
- Install physical barriers around the pool to limit access.
    1. Fences and walls should be at least 4-feet high and installed completely around the pool.
    2. Gates should be self-closing and self-latching. The latch should be out of reach of small children.
- If your house forms one side of the barrier for the pool, doors leading from the house to the pool should be protected with alarms that sound when the doors are unexpectedly opened. Or, use a power safety cover, a motor-powered barrier placed over the water area, to prevent access by young children.
- For above-ground pools, steps and ladders to the pool should be secured or removed when the pool is not in use.

Pool and Spa Entrapment Dangers

- Never use a pool or spa with a missing or broken drain cover. Be sure a newer, safer drain cover is in place. The new drain covers are usually dome-shaped instead of flat.

- Consider installing a Safety Vacuum Release System (SVRS), a device that automatically shuts off a pump if a blockage is detected.
- Have a professional regularly inspect your pool or spa for entanglement hazards.
- Plainly mark the location of the electrical cut-off switch for the pool or spa pump.
- If someone is trapped against a drain, shut off the pump immediately. Instead of trying to pull the person away from the powerful suction, pry a hand between the drain and the person's body to break the seal

Beach Safety

The Ocean

Most of the time, you don't even notice the bare flagpoles dotting the dunes up and down the coast. But when the ocean is too rough for swimming, there's no way you can miss the red flags hoisted all along the beach. If red flags are flying, do not go into the water at all. Not only will the ocean be too dangerous for swimming or wading, it is against the law to swim during a red-flag warning. You could be fined for going into the water.

The flags signify not only dangerous waves, but deadly rip currents as well. Churning water can easily knock you down, and reports of broken bones are not uncommon. Rough water also produces floating debris that seems to come from nowhere. We've seen adult men wading in knee-deep water knocked down by powerful waves and dragged by rip currents on red-flag days. In short, even if you see surfers in the water, stay out while the flags are flying, and caution children to keep well away from the tide line. Keep in mind, too, that if you go into the water while the flags are flying and need rescuing, you are jeopardizing not only your life but also the lifeguard's life when he or she has to come in after you.

Water Sense

- Never swim alone.
- Never swim at night.
- Observe the surf before going in the water, looking for potentially dangerous currents.
- Non-swimmers should stay out of the water and wear life jackets if they're going to be near the water.
- Swim in areas with on-duty lifeguards, or use extreme care.
- Keep non-swimming children well above the marks of the highest waves.
- Keep an eye on children at all times, and teach them never to turn their backs on the waves while they play at water's edge.
- Don't swim near anglers or deployed fishing lines.
- Stay 300 feet away from fishing piers.
- Watch out for surfers and give them plenty of room.

Losing Control in the Waves

If a wave crashes down on you while you are surfing or swimming and you find yourself being tumbled in bubbles and sand like a sheet in a washing machine, don't try to struggle to the surface against it. Curl into a ball, or just go limp and float. The wave will take you to the beach, or you can just swim to the surface when it passes.

Backwash Current

A backwash current on a steeply sloping beach can pull you toward deeper water, but its power is swiftly checked by incoming waves. To escape this current, swim straight toward shore if you're a strong swimmer. If you're not, don't panic; wait and float until the current stops, then swim in.

Rip Currents

Rip currents often occur where there's a break in a submerged sandbar. Water trapped between the sandbar and the beach rushes out through the breach, sometimes sweeping swimmers out with it. You can see a rip; it's choppy, turbulent, often discolored water that looks deeper than the water around it. If you are caught in a rip, don't try to swim against the current. Instead, swim across the current, parallel to the shore, and slowly work your way back to the beach at an angle. Try to remain calm. Panic will only sap the energy you need to swim out of the rip.

Undertow

When a wave comes up on the beach and breaks, the water must run back down to the sea. This is undertow. It sucks at your ankles from small waves, but in heavy surf the undertow can knock you off your feet and carry you offshore. If you're carried out, don't resist. Let the undertow take you out until it subsides. It will only be a few yards. The next wave will help push you shoreward again.

<u>Heat Exhaustion</u>

Heat-related illness can affect anyone not used to hot weather, especially when it's combined with high humidity. <u>Those especially at risk:</u>

- Infants, young children, elderly and pets
- Individuals with heart or circulatory problems or other long-term illness
- Employees working in the heat

- Athletes and people who like to exercise (especially beginners)
- Individuals taking certain medications that alter sweat production
- Alcoholics and drug abusers

Heatstroke is the most serious and life-threatening heat-related illness. In certain circumstances, your body can build up too much heat, your temperature may rise to life-threatening levels, and you can become delirious or lose consciousness. If you do not rid your body of excess heat fast enough, it "cooks" the brain and other vital organs. It is often fatal, and those who do survive may have permanent damage to their vital organs.

Symptoms of heatstroke:

- The victim's body feels extremely hot when touched.
- Altered mental status (behavior) ranging from slight confusion and disorientation to coma.
- Conscious victims usually become irrational, agitated, or even aggressive and may have seizures.
- In severe heatstroke, the victim can go into a coma in less than one hour. The longer the coma lasts, the lower the chance for survival.

What to do:

- Move person to a half-sitting position in the shade.
- Call for emergency medical help immediately.
- If humidity is below 75%, spray victim with water and vigorously fan. If humidity above 75%, apply ice packs on neck, armpits or groin.

Heat exhaustion is characterized by heavy perspiration with normal or slightly above normal body temperatures. It is caused by water or salt depletion or both (severe dehydration). Heat exhaustion affects workers and athletes who do not drink enough fluids while working or exercising in hot environments.

Symptoms of heat exhaustion include:

- Severe thirst, fatigue, headache, nausea, vomiting and sometimes diarrhea.
- The affected person often mistakenly believes he or she has the flu.
- Uncontrolled heat exhaustion can evolve into heatstroke.

Other symptoms:

- Profuse sweating
- Clammy or pale skin
- Dizziness
- Rapid pulse
- Normal or slightly above normal body temperature

What to do:

- Sit or lie down in the shade.
- Drink cool, lightly salted water or sports drink.
- If persistent, gently apply wet towels and call for emergency medical help.

Heat cramps are painful muscular spasms that occur suddenly and affect legs and/or abdominal muscles. They usually happen after physical activity in people who sweat a lot or have not had enough fluids. Victims may be drinking water without adequate salt content.

What to do:

- Sit or lie down in the shade.
- Drink cool, lightly salted water or sports drink.
- Stretch affected muscles.

Sun protection habits include:

- Limit sun exposure during the hours when the sun's rays are the strongest, 10am to 4pm.
- Seek shade whenever possible.
- Wear a wide-brimmed hat, sunglasses, and long-sleeved, tightly woven clothing.
- Use broad-spectrum sunscreens whose active ingredients block UVA and UVB rays. They should be applied liberally and evenly before going out into the sun and should be applied frequently, especially after swimming.
- Avoid tanning salons. Artificial UV radiation is just as bad for your skin as sunlight.
- Limit exposure to the reflective surfaces like snow and water. UV rays can be reflected off of sand, tile, water, snow, and buildings.

Don't forget the Sunscreen!

Teachable Moments

Empowering your child with safety techniques will help build their self-confidence and give them the strength to use these tools to be safe. Practice what you teach with a variety of scenarios and see how your children will react. Repetition is KEY.

Now that your child knows about various forms of danger and criminals, it's extremely important for them (and us as adults, too) to remember as much as possible about our predator. The most important features to remember are ones that cannot change quickly:

- Gender
- Skin Tone
- Size (height and weight)
- Hair length, color and texture

To help you and your child remember these items, play a game. While in public, select a person to look at for a few seconds. Turn around and ask the child what they remember about the person you picked. Once you can identify these features easily, move on to more specific features. Police will ask for these pieces of information:

- Glasses
- Hair length
- Age
- Clothing worn
- Identifying marks on body such as scars or tattoos
- For male, any facial hair

If you practice these things in a non-threatening environment, it will become easier each time it's done and pretty soon it will become second nature.

Another game you should play with your child, which will benefit you both, is one that will help you identify vehicles. This is as important as identifying the person involved:

- The make and model of the car (hard for children to remember)
- Vehicle color
- Vehicle type (van, pickup, 2 door, 4 door, SUV)

- The license plate number
- Hard top vs convertible
- Sliding door vs opening doors
- Hatchback or tailgate
- Tinted windows
- Any distinguishing marks like dents, rust marks, bumper stickers, special tire rims that stand out

So how do you recognize a license plate number? It's not as difficult as you might think. When I was a child my grandparents remembered their license plate this way – Grover, Yellow, Rose – 466 (their last name, Grover; and my grandmother's favorite flower – Yellow Rose). They have been gone 10 years now and I still remember their plate number! For my children to remember my plate number we have made up words that were fun, meaningful and made silly sentences. I realize different states use different sequences of numbers and letters. Yet, this technique can still work if learned and practiced repetitively in a safe, fun environment.

Certain letters of the alphabet can sound alike. Even law enforcement has problems understanding certain letters over their radio communication. To avoid confusion, they use a Phonetic Alphabet (my daughter learned these in school at her Police Teen Academy which was hosted by the school's SRO – the goal of this great program was to provide teens a dynamic experience of the role and duties of a police officer, with emphasis on serving and protecting all citizens. The long-term goal was to leave teens with the lasting impression that we all have policing duties and we arc all responsible for the safety of others! We need more of these…):

A= Adam	N= Nora
B= Boy or Boston	O= Ocean

C=Charles	P= Paul
D=David	Q= Queen
E=Edward	R= Robert
F=Frank	S= Sam
G=George	T= Tom
H= Henry	U= Union
I= Ida	V= Victor
J= John	W= William
K= King	X= X-ray
L= Lincoln	Y= Young
M= Mary	Z= Zebra

What to do if Your Child is Ever Lost

My daughter was 7, my son 3. We were leaving the shopping mall. We were walking from the restroom out the doors to the parking lot – a total of maybe thirty feet at the most. My children were right in front of me holding hands. I looked down to rearrange the bags in my hands. I looked up and my son was gone. My daughter didn't remember letting go of his hand. Panic set in and my heart was in my throat. He was found 10 minutes later in the clothes rack playing "hide and seek" with us.

We were in Lowe's shopping with friends – they had two boys the same age as my kids. We stopped to ask a "Handyman" a question about bathrooms. Within seconds, her younger son was gone. We couldn't find him any where. Their wonderful store policy (Code Adam) was to close all the doors and keep everyone inside until the child was located. Everyone pitched in looking – restrooms, up and down each isle, under items, etc. This was a big store with a lot of places to hide a small child. His name was called over the loud speaker. Apparently, he was afraid to come out of hiding because he thought he was now in trouble. One hour later, we located him hiding inside one of the display cabinets playing. The fear we experienced was immeasurable.

Luckily, like the above stories, a child is normally lost for just a few seconds or minutes. Still, that amount of time seems like forever for the parent who is frantically searching.

You can't keep your eye on your child every second, as hard as we try. Therefore, you must plan ahead to make sure you find your child fast if he or she is ever lost at a ball field, amusement park, the mall, or any other public place. Children won't know what to do when they're lost unless you tell them ahead of time. It will be reassuring for you both to know you have a "lost and found" plan if you are ever separated.

If your child is ever lost, parents should:

1. Act IMMEDIATELY – time is crucial
2. Enlist help from security guards, police, store managers or whomever you can get to help you look for your child
3. Give the authorities an accurate description of your child. Hair/eye color, Height, Weight, Clothing dressed in, any distinguishing marks (moles, scars, etc). You should have a new up to date picture of your child with you.
4. Check every logical location and fan out. If you taught your child to stay in the area where you were separated, then you can concentrate your search there. Or better yet, if you and your child have agreed on a meeting place if you should become separated, go there but be sure someone stays is the spot where you last saw your child in case they show back up there.
5. If at home, check your house from top to bottom,

move on to the neighborhood and try checking with all of your child's friends. Then look in or call places he or she normally spends time.

6. Retrace the child's last known steps

Plan ahead:

- If at a stadium or auditorium, write the child's section and seat number on the back of his/her hand
- Dress your child in bright or distinctive clothing so they will stand out in a crowd.
- Thoroughly discuss with your child what to do if they become lost. In public places, agree on a meeting spot if you are separated (as an adult, I still do this when shopping with my mother!)
- When you find the child, remember this is not the time to reprimand him for getting lost. Instead, let him know you are glad to see him and praise him / her for being smart and brave.

(This information was written, in part, from material published by the National Center for Missing and Exploited Children: after you have reported your child missing to law enforcement, call the **National Center for Missing & Exploited Children** on their toll-free telephone number: **1-800-THE-LOST (1-800-843-5678).**)

How Youth Can Help Combat Violence

When youthful energy is channeled through community service, amazing things happen: parks are cleaned up, children learn about the dangers of drug abuse, an elderly person gains a companion, affordable housing is built, and teenagers confront tough questions about personal responsibility. Young people learn the elements of leadership and the principles of teamwork while building their own self worth. Youth are capable of doing much more than adults usually ask—or allow—them to do. But if young people are to become responsible adults, they should be engaged in the community right now; they should not wait until they reach 18. Taking the lead in designing and carrying out solutions to community problems can give young people a sense of competence and confidence that extends into adulthood. Although adults can lend support, youth can—and should—take the lead whenever possible.

What Can Youth Bring to the Prevention of Crime and Violence?

Youth have much to contribute:
- Youth have a keen awareness of the effects of crime on the community.
- Youth have firsthand knowledge of the feeling of vulnerability; they are in the age group that is most victimized by crime.
- In many cases, they know where the problems are.
- They have both idealism and creativity.
- They are willing to take risks.
- They have an enormous amount of energy.
- They want to be part of a group.

NOTES

5 IMPORTANT THINGS I LEARNED FROM THIS SECTION:

1. _____

2. _____

3. _____

4. _____

5. _____

IMMEDIATE ACTION STEPS THAT I WILL TAKE TODAY! :

_____

_____

_____

_____

_____

_____

_____

_____

_____

_____

_____

PART II

Protect U –
Unique Challenges Of
Safety On Campus

Ensuring Safety On and Off Campus

-trust your strengths and weaknesses
-determine when a threat is real
-stay centered in a bad situation
-dress for safety
-avoid looking like a victim
-avoid sexual predators and scam artists

Safety Tips for College Students / Young Adults –

College should be a time of great exploration. However, with more dangers developing every school year – from hazing to late-night parties to predators on campus – parents are getting more than a case of "empty nest" syndrome. Many parents panic when their child makes the big move, but panicking doesn't solve any problems. By learning and teaching their teen precautions, parents can keep their child out of harm's way during collegiate years away from home.

Teens are the victims of property and personal crimes more than any other group. They are at risk because they go out more frequently, often at night, and tend to overlook personal safety rules. Law enforcement authorities estimate that up to 90% of all crime could be prevented if people use basic safety measures

- Freshmen should "respectfully decline" to have photo and personal information published for distribution to the campus community. Fraternities and upperclassmen and others with access have abused this type of publication to "target" naive freshmen.

- Study the campus and neighborhood with respect to routes between your residence and class/activity schedule. Know where emergency phones are located and carry a cell phone.

- Share your class/activities schedule with parents and a network of close friends, effectively creating a type of "buddy" system. Give network telephone numbers to your parents, advisors, and friends.

- Always travel in groups. Use a shuttle service after dark. Never walk alone at night. Avoid "shortcuts" and don't be the last person out of the library at night.

- Survey the campus, academic buildings, residence halls, and other facilities while classes are in session and after dark to see that buildings, walkways, quadrangles and parking lots are adequately secured, lit and patrolled. Are emergency phones, escorts, and shuttle services adequate?

To gauge the social scene, drive down fraternity row on weekend nights and stroll through the student hangouts. Are people behaving responsibly, or does the situation seem reckless and potentially dangerous? Remember, alcohol and/or drug abuse is involved in about 90% of campus crime. Carefully evaluate off-campus student apartment complexes and fraternity houses if you plan to live off-campus.

- Do not give your name and address to strangers.
- Do not give out personal information over the telephone to people you do not know. (SS #, credit card #'s, driver's license #'s, address, etc.)

- When leaving your residence hall, campus, etc., let someone know where you are going.
- Walk with a friend. It is much less likely that something will happen if there are two of you.
- Never walk alone at night. Many college security and safety departments offer an escort service that provides you with the assurance of safe travel on campus.
- Have your key ready to open your car doors, especially at night. Your keys can be a defensive weapon.
- Look inside your car before entering; also check the vehicle for possible break-ins. Assailants sometimes hide in the back seat of a vehicle or even under it.
- Personal property should never be left unattended, even if it is only for a few minutes. Remember, take it with you or lock it up. Take your books and book bags to your table when you go to eat and don't leave your purse, wallet, or other valuables unattended.
- Always make sure that the office or classroom door is locked if you should be working or studying late. Remember; never prop any door open for someone else.
- You should report all incidents involving vandalism, theft, damage or persons in the residence hall that are not escorted or are suspicious in nature.
- When leaving your residence hall room, whether it is to visit a next-door neighbor or to use the restroom, always lock the door and take the key. Lock your door, even if you only plan on being gone a few minutes.
- Avoid keeping high value items and large amounts of cash in your residence. For valued items you do keep on hand, keep them out of sight and well

hidden. The same procedure applies to your credit card, checkbook, and your unused check supply as well.

- Engrave items of value and be sure to maintain a record of serial numbers of such items as personal computers, TVs, radios, stereos, answering machines, cameras, etc. A copy of this record should also be maintained at another offsite location. You should engrave your driver's license # and state on items. Driver's license #'s are easier for police to track.

- Don't let strangers into the building or allow them to "tailgate" or follow you through after you open the door.

- Do not lend your room key, residence hall key or give out the residence hall door combination. The residence hall is like your home, nobody should enter without you wanting them there. These are college violations.

- Entrance doors to the residence halls should never be propped open. The locks are designed to allow only residence of the hall to have access. Propping doors open will allow non-residences to enter, jeopardizing your safety and that of everyone else.

- All visitors, student and non-student, are required at all times to be escorted while in a residence hall by the person they are visiting.

- All visitors are to be escorted out of the residence halls when leaving.

- All suspicious person(s) need to be reported immediately to your RA, RD or Security.

- All crimes need to be reported immediately to your RA, RD or Security.

- Do not leave notes on your door that you are not there. That is an invitation for some unwanted person to enter your room.

- Keep your shades drawn when changing clothes or retiring for the night.
- Purchase locking devices if you have your own computer and printer in your room.
- Carry a non-lethal weapon like Mace/Pepper spray for "distance" protection

Apartment Safety Tips

Do you think you, your roommate/family, and your belongings are safe in your apartment? Are you sure? Do you know what you should be looking for when you look for an apartment or analyze your home security?

- Get to know both your neighbors and the neighborhood. Be aware of what's happening in the area, especially if any of your neighbors have been victims of burglary
- Make sure there is adequate lighting in all exterior areas of the complex. If you believe there is an area that needs more light, notify the landlord, and ask neighbors to do the same. Your landlord is required by law to provide you with a safe environment. Also notify the maintenance office immediately if you notice burnt out bulbs in any lights in exterior or common areas.
- Make sure your door has a dead bolt in addition to any knob lock. Don't rely on either locks in knobs or on chains. Your door should also have a peephole (if you have children, consider getting one at their height, too). You can ask the landlord to replace or re-key your dead bolt and install a peephole. If he won't do it, see about doing it at your own expense (don't forget to give a key to the landlord if you are

required to under the lease).

- If you have a security system in the building – use it. Don't ever buzz strangers into the building or allow strangers to enter the building when you are entering or leaving.
- Be careful when using laundry or other common facilities after dark. Consider doing laundry, swimming, working out, etc. with a buddy. If these facilities have locking doors, make sure they are locked, and don't let anyone in who doesn't have a key.
- Make sure any windows accessible from the ground, balconies, or fire escapes have stops to prevent them opening enough to let a person through. A long screw in the frame is enough to stop a window from opening more than a couple of inches while still allowing ventilation.
- If you have a sliding glass door, use a stop of some sort in the track to keep the door from opening more than a few inches (a steel or wooden dowel is inexpensive and generally effective). You should also install screws in the frame to prevent the entire door from being removed.
- Make sure you have adequate smoke detectors, especially outside the kitchen and bedrooms. Check your detectors regularly and replace batteries at least twice a year. Make sure any necessary carbon monoxide or natural gas detectors are also working and maintained.
- Purchase fire extinguishers. There should be one accessible from the bedrooms, and one in the kitchen. Ideally the extinguishers should be rated ABC (for all three major types of fire) – the extinguisher in the kitchen should have a definite B rating (for grease and other flammable liquids).

- Know all routes of escape from your apartment in case of fire. Inexpensive collapsible ladders by bedroom windows will ensure escape should a fire block other exits. Make sure your entire room/family can exit directly from your apartment to the outdoors, and practice.
- Don't advertise your absence by leaving notes for maintenance personnel, children, neighbors, etc., on your door or mailbox.
- Single women should never have their full names listed in the phone book or posted on buzzers or mailboxes. Try to get your neighbors to all agree to use initials on buzzers and mailboxes. If you live alone, try putting two initials on the buzzer.
- If you are living alone or a single mother, leave a message on your answering machine that says "We can't answer the phone right now, but we will be back to you soon". Convey the message that you don't live alone. Or have a male friend tape your message for you.
- Don't hide a spare key outside. If you want, find a neighbor you trust and make a deal to keep each other's spare keys. Having to pay a locksmith to get you in is still cheaper than losing your valuables when a thief finds the key.
- Don't list your entire address in the phone book – list only a street name or just the town or city. Reverse listings can allow thieves to find your phone number and full name from your address.
- Get renters insurance. If anything were to happen, you'd at least be able to replace your belongings.
- Keep an inventory of your valuables. Photographs of expensive jewelry and serial numbers of all electronic and computer equipment should be kept in a fireproof safe or safe deposit box. Etching your

driver's license number on your electronics can identify them in the case of theft (many police departments offer this etching as a free service).

- Talk to your local police department about having a security check – many will do them for free.
- Consider starting a neighborhood watch program in your complex or community.
- If you are really concerned, there are a number of wireless home security systems perfect for apartment dwellers.

Reduce Your Risks While Traveling and At Work

- At night, have someone walk you to your car or bus stop. Avoid isolated areas at work. Lock up your valuables. Report anyone who seems suspicious. Both sexes can be victims of sexual harassment. If sexually harassed (offensive language, literature or actions), tell the harasser not to do it again. Write down the incident. If it happens again, tell a supervisor; if you get no help, contact the Equal Employment Opportunity Commission (EEOC). To learn more about your rights and safety at work visit:
  - National Institute for Occupational Safety and Health website at **http://www.cdc.gov/niosh/adoldoc.html.**
  - U.S. Department of Labor – YouthRules! Website at **http://www.youthrules.dol.gov/teens/defa ult.htm**
- On public transportation, have your fare ready; use well-lit, busy stops; sit near driver or by a group. If danger arises, attempt to move closer to the driver; alert driver of the problem. If driving lock your car when you get in and out; park in well-lit, busy

areas; check in and around your car before entering. If your vehicle breaks down use emergency flashers; contact the police and your roadside assistance provider, tie a white cloth to the door; stay inside locked car; place a "call police" sign in the window, through slightly open window ask anyone who stops to call for help. For more information on transportation safety issues go to the

  o National Highway Traffic Safety Administration website at **http://www.nhtsa.gov.**

PAR - TEEEEE....

Pledging for sororities and fraternities has always been a part of the college life. But some students are waking up with more than just a hangover after a night of pledging, including signs of physical abuse. The culprit is called hazing, a harmful initiation process that has become far too common on college campuses among those in a certain group and those who will do anything to be in that group.

Hazing comes in many forms. Typically, it includes:

- Binge drinking
- Paddling
- Spitting
- Forcing participants to over eat
- Beating
- Mental or physical intimidation

Hazing activities are very hard to categorize and/or minimize. However, any college student's best defense is to know how to handle situations before they arise. Teach your child to be smart about it. If someone is trying to make your child do something your child doesn't want to do, your child should know his or her limits. Maybe you want your child to avoid the situation entirely, or maybe you want your child to negotiate with the hazers. You don't want your child to lose the respect of his or her peers, but you want your child to get out of dangerous situations before it is too late. Use your good judgment and pass that on to your child.

Safe Partying

Social activities in college are not simply restricted to the glee club. Partying is a large part of collegiate life on weekends, and even the most sheltered of children will experiment. Your job should be to remind your kids that it is possible to be safe and still have a good time. If you know your child is partying, don't feel like you need to stop them from doing so. Especially when they are away, they may take the liberty to do what they want anyway. Instead, talk to him or her about how to throw a safe party. Then encourage your child to spread that knowledge to his or her friends. Communicate to your child that you just want them to be safe so they can enjoy the other aspects of college life.

Weekend and Party Safety Issues

- Don't do *ANYTHING* that makes you feel uncomfortable. People won't look down on you for saying "no," and if they do, they're not worth your time.
- Don't accept any food or drinks from someone you don't completely trust.
- Never leave your drink unattended.
- Don't drink from punch bowls where you don't know what has been put into it.

- Make sure you have a safe way to get home.
- Make sure your parents, roommate, etc… know where you are.
- Beware of drugs like "the date rape drug." Some drugs can be hard to detect, and have very serious affects.
- Try to keep parties under control, even if it comes to you calling the police.
- Act responsibly. If you get caught doing something illegal, not only will you have to face the consequences, if you're underage, your parents or guardians could also be held responsible.
- Adopt the "buddy system." Go to a party with a friend, and make sure you leave with that friend.
- Don't drive while intoxicated, and don't allow a friend to drive while under the influence of any substance.
- Don't hesitate to call 911 if there is a medical emergency

Club Drugs

Use of "Club Drugs", especially GHB (Gamma-hydroxy butyrate) and MDMA (methylenedioxymethamphetamine also known as "ecstasy", "blue lips", "blue kisses", "white dove", "E", "X" and "XTC") continue to be reported across the country.

The following Q&A information is courtesy of Officer Scott Roach – Education Coordinator, MO. Highway Safety.

The Date Rape Drug

'GHB' Q and A

What is it?

GHB, or gamma-hydroxy butyrate, is a central nervous system depressant that is abused for its intoxicating effects. There are more *than 80* known names for GHB and its equally deadly analogs.

> GHB: AKA --- G, Jib, Scoop, Liquid E, Liquid X, Woman's Viagra, Grievous Bodily Harm, Easy Lay, Gamma 10, Gook, Liquid X, Liquid E, Liquid G, Georgia Home Boy, Scoop, Salty Water, GH Buddy, Aminos, Blue Nitro, Blue Thunder, Thunder Nectar, Renewtrient, Revivarant, Remforce, Firewater, Invigorate, Xyrem (research product), Sodium Oxybate, Fantasy & One4B (NZ), Gina, Swirl, Tranquili G, Midnight Blue, Verve, Rejoov, Somax, SomatoPro, Flower Power, Puritech, Alcover, G-riffick, Eclipse, GHGold, Soap, Vita G, Dormir, Enliven, FX, Serenity, Inner G, Zen, White Magic Cleaner, Weight Belt Cleaner, Ink Jet Cartridge Cleaner, Plant Food, Fingernail Polish Remover, Paint Stripper, Somatomax, Cherry Meth, Fantasy, Organic Quaalude, Nature's Quaalude, and Zonked.. – THE LIST GOES ON AND ON….

Don't be fooled – These are NOT safe, natural ways to get high, get some sleep, get buff, relieve anxiety, enhance sexual feelings, combat aging or fight stress or depression. **Beware…..... it's what you *don't* know that can kill you – or someone you love.**

Rohypnol (Flunitrazepam) is a tranquilizer developed in the 1960s and early 1970s by Hoffman-La Roche, Inc., and first marketed under the trade name Rohypnol in Switzerland in 1975. Rohypnol is 10 to 20 times more potent than Valium (diazepam). This class of drugs is used to treat anxiety, convulsions, muscle tension and sleep disorders. Its powerful sedative effects can last up to 12 hours, with some residual effects occurring as long as 24 hours later. Low doses of Rohypnol may cause drowsiness, dizziness, motor in-coordination, memory loss, gastrointestinal upsets, headache, reduced blood pressure, visual disturbances, dry mouth, and hangover. Higher doses can cause coma, respiratory depression, and even death.

Rohypnol impairs mental judgment and reaction time, and individuals who drive under its influence increase their chances of automobile accidents. Law enforcement officers have frequently reported observing severely impaired driving ability in motorists who have used Rohypnol along with small amounts of alcohol. The effects of Rohypnol, also referred to as "Rophies," "Roofies," "Ropes," and "Roach-2," are similar to alcohol intoxication, and there are three distinct patterns of abuse of this drug; alone for its intoxicating effects; in combination with other drugs; and for the purpose of rape.

How is it used?

GHB is consumed orally in capsule form or as a grainy, white to sandy-colored powder. Powdered GHB is often dissolved in liquids like water or alcoholic beverages and then consumed. However, it is most frequently sold as a slightly salty, clear liquid in small bottles where users pay by the capful or by the teaspoon. Most GHB is created in clandestine laboratories where purity and quality cannot be guaranteed. Often substituted for Ecstasy, another club drug, a capful may cost the user $3 to $5 per dose. GHB is also used as a sedative to come down off stimulants like ephedrine, Ecstasy, speed, or cocaine

What are its effects?

The effects of GHB are heavily affected by one's body weight, interactions with other chemicals, and one's individual reaction. Some people find GHB to be useful for treating insomnia, others use it as part of the process of breaking alcohol addiction and some use it as an alcohol replacement.

Why is it a "date rape drug?"

GHB produces intoxication followed by deep sedation. Once ingested, the drug will begin to take effect in 15 minutes to an hour, lasting one to three hours. Sexual predators and street gangs take advantage of the sedative and memory loss effects of GHB/ Rohypnol to incapacitate women and commit sexual assault. The severe mental incapacitation, along with the amnesia produced by GHB/Rohypnol, makes it difficult, if not altogether impossible, for the rape victim to recall the circumstances surrounding her sexual assault. The use of Rohypnol to commit sexual assault has earned it the street names of the "Forget Pill," the "Date-Rape Drug," "Trip-and-Fall," and "Mind-Erasers." Adding to the complexity of the problem of Rohypnol/GHB use in the commission of rape, is the victim's difficulty in remembering facts surrounding the incident, compounding the problem of successful rape prosecution for law enforcement agencies. In Texas, street gangs have been known to administer Rohypol to females in order to commit gang rape as part of initiation into the gang.

GHB can cause nausea, vomiting, delusions, depression, vertigo, visual disturbances, seizures, respiratory distress, loss of consciousness, amnesia, and coma. When combined with alcohol and other drugs, the potential for deadly overdoses escalates rapidly. Numerous overdoses nationwide have required emergency room treatment and mechanical assistance to breathe.

Where can it be purchased?

Clubs, Raves, Student Undergrounds, but most easily....ONLINE!

What Are Raves?

"Raves" are high energy, all-night dances that feature hard pounding techno-music and flashing laser lights. Raves are found in most metropolitan areas and, increasingly, in rural areas throughout the country. The parties are held in permanent dance clubs, abandoned warehouses, open fields, or empty buildings. Raves are frequently advertised as "alcohol free" parties with hired security personnel. Internet sites often advertise these events as "safe" and "drug free." However, they are dangerously over crowded parties where your child can be exposed to rampant drug use and a high-crime environment. Numerous overdoses are documented at these events. Because some club drugs are colorless, odorless, and tasteless, they can be added without detection to beverages by individuals who want to intoxicate or sedate others in order to commit sexual assaults. Rave promoters capitalize on the effects of club drugs. Bottled water and sports drinks are sold at Raves, often at inflated prices, to manage hyperthermia and dehydration. Also found are pacifiers to prevent involuntary teeth clenching, menthol nasal inhalers, surgical masks, chemical lights, and neon glow sticks to increase sensory perception and enhance the Rave experience. Cool down rooms are provided, usually at a cost, as a place to cool off due to increased body temperature of the drug user. Don't risk your child's health and safety. Ask questions about where he or she is going and see it for yourself.

- One important lesson here – never leave your drink unattended at bars or parties and don't accept a mixed drink at a party from someone you don't know.

Other Drugs That Parents Should Be Aware Of That Are Being Used:

- *Cocaine* – remains the Nation's dominant drug problem
- *Heroin* – street informants indicate a steady increase in young buyers. Purity has gone up while price has declined. New and young users are reportedly progressing from snorting to injecting.
- *Marijuana* – Now accounts for more than 10 % of total Emergency Department mentions in 12 cities (Atlanta, Boston, Dallas, Detroit, Los Angeles, Miami, New Orleans, Philadelphia, St Louis, San Diego and Washington DC). It is commonly combined with Crack, PCP, PCP with formaldehyde and with psilocybin mushrooms.
- *Stimulants – Methamphetamine* remains concentrated in the West and injecting remains the primary route of administration in many areas but that seems to be declining as snorting and smoking the product has increased. Street names: Speed, Ice, Chalk, Meth, Crystal, Crank, Fire, Glass
- A central nervous system stimulant, often found in pill, capsule, or powder form, which can be snorted, injected, or smoked.
  Effects:
  1. Displays signs of agitation, excited speech, lack of appetite, and increased physical activity. Often results in drastic weight loss, violence, psychotic behavior, paranoia, and sometimes damage to the heart or nervous system

- *Ketamine ("Special K" or "Vitamin K")* is injected intramuscularly by young, white, middle-class clients; converted into a white powder and snorted; smoked or mixed in beverages – it has been responsible for deaths in New Orleans and San Diego. Street names: Special K, K, Vitamin K, Cat Valium. An injectable anesthetic used primarily by veterinarians, found either in liquid form or as a white powder that can be snorted or smoked, sometimes with marijuana.
  Effects:
  1. Causes reactions similar to those of PCP, a hallucinatory drug.
  2. Results in impaired attention, learning, and memory function. In larger doses, it may cause delirium, amnesia, impaired motor function, high blood pressure, and depression.

- *Clonazepam (Klonopin or Rivotril) and Alprazolam (Xanax)* have recently been mentioned in more hospital emergencies. Among youth in Miami, "Xanax Candy Bars" have caused several medical emergencies. In many cases, these benzodiazepines are used to reduce "the edge" from cocaine and meth.

- *Adderall* parties are becoming a popular college campus past time as well – the stimulant helps keep the students awake (commonly used for ADHD)

- *More and more teens are moving away from illicit drugs due to education, parental pressures and awareness but they are now moving to the unsupervised and addictive use of prescription products such as pain killers*

Know the Signs:

Effects of stimulant club drugs, such as MDMA and

Methamphetamine:

- Increased heart rate
- Convulsions
- Extreme rise in body temperature
- Uncontrollable movements
- Insomnia
- Impaired speech
- Dehydration
- High blood pressure
- Grinding teeth

Effects of sedative/hallucinogenic club drugs, such as GHB, Ketamine, LSD, and Rohypnol:

- Slow breathing
- Decreased heart rate (Except LSD)
- Respiratory problems
- Intoxication
- Drowsiness
- Confusion
- Tremors
- Nausea

Effects common to all club drugs can include anxiety, panic, depression, euphoria, loss of memory, hallucinations, and psychotic behavior. Drugs, traces of drugs, and drug paraphernalia are direct evidence of drug abuse. Pacifiers, menthol inhalers, surgical masks, and other such items could also be considered indicators (not an all inclusive list):

Other signs of drug use:

- Reckless behavior
- Change in friends

- No concern about the future
- Neglected appearance and/or hygiene
- Poor self image
- Violent outbursts
- Frequent use of eye drops or wash
- Running away
- Skin abrasions/lesions
- Always asking for money and/or borrowing money
- Missing valuables
- Glassy / Red eyes
- Verbally abusive / disrespectful to parents and authority figures
- Sneaky behavior

Why do kids use drugs?

Understanding the teenage perspective holds important keys. There are many pressures teens deal with on a daily basis. When kids are asked why they began using drugs, they do not look outward to outside influences. Rather their reasons include those similar to the following responses:

- They want to fit in, to feel part of the group
- To rebel against adult authority
- To escape their problems
- To hide their feelings of inadequacy and low self esteem
- The thrill and excitement
- Wanting to feel grown up

Never Underestimate The Number One Drug Of Choice In America – Alcohol

If you think it can't happen to you, look around. Check your school year book for the last 10 years. How many pages are dedicated to a student who was killed in a drunk-driving accident? Ask the people you know, how many bad things have happened to them when they or someone else was drinking. You don't even have to be the one drinking. Most teen-aged deaths are caused to passengers when the driver was impaired by alcohol.

The negative effects of teen drug use are undeniable and obvious. When considering those negative effects, it is alarming to see some of the actual statistics concerning the amount of teen drug use in high schools and middle schools. In addition, many parents felt that their teen's alcohol use was okay because it wasn't a harder drug like crack, or heroine. However, it should be noted that alcohol kills five times more teenagers than all other drugs combined (usually through accidents)! Below are just a few of alarming statistics associated with teen drug use and the effects of alcohol on teenagers.

- Illicit teen drug use as of 2003.
- * 8th grade -- 30.3%
- * 10th grade -- 44.9%
- * 12th grade -- 52.8%
- Underage drinking costs the United States more than $58 billion dollars annually, enough for a new state of the art computer for every student.
- In the last thirty days 50% of teenagers report drinking with 32% being drunk on at least one occasion.
- Alcohol is the number one drug of choice for teenagers
- Alcohol related car crashes are the number one leading cause of death among teenagers – (could you live with yourself if you were responsible for killing someone else?)
- Alcohol changes your depth perception and slurs

your speech
- Alcohol causes you to loose your inhibitions. Your judgment is impaired and bad things can happen like: automobile crashes, violence, unwanted pregnancy, sexual transmission of diseases or rape
- A significant portion of violent crimes and vandalisms among and by youth involve alcohol
- Alcohol can cost you your freedom – grounding by parents, loss of driver's license, jail time
- You can get sick and die from alcohol poisoning
- Poor grades may be the result of alcohol usage.
- One beer, One glass of wine and One shot of whiskey all have the same amount of alcohol
- Drinking alcohol does not quench your thirst – it causes dehydration
- **8 young people die in alcohol related crashes EVERY DAY**

Remember, no one ever says they want to grow up to be an alcoholic. It is a slow, gradual process and it has no boundaries for those affected. It is not just the bum (these account for only 3 – 5% of alcoholics) on the street who becomes an alcoholic. It affects many professionals and many times costs them their jobs, families and overall livelihood. The younger you start drinking the more likely it will become an addiction and life long problem. It may seem like a fun thing to do but it ruins lives and it's easier to never start (like cigarettes) than it is to quit! Today, a DWI will not only hurt your driving record but it will affect your chances on obtaining certain jobs in the future and will cost you up to $10,000 with court / legal fees. A 28 day program for rehabilitation costs on average $35,000 and isn't covered by most insurance plans. In addition to the fact that drinking under age is illegal and you might kill someone besides yourself, can you afford these additional expenditures and consequences?

Rise In Prescription Drug Usage Among Teens

Today teenagers are not using as much cocaine, crack, LSD, and ecstasy as the teenagers of the 1960's. Kids have found other ways and means to get high; painkillers and other prescription drugs are being abused at record levels. This up coming generation of teens has been given the name "Generation Rx."

Teens are often getting caught raiding their parent's or grandparent's medicine cabinets in order to get high. For the first time, national studies show that today's teens are more likely to have abused a prescription painkiller than any illicit drug.

Teenagers may get involved with prescription drugs in various ways. The experimental stage can be very dangerous, because kids often don't see the link between their actions today the consequences of their actions tomorrow.

Most teens have a tendency to feel indestructible and immune to the problems that others experience. Some teens will experiment and stop, while others may continue to use occasionally without any significant problem. Then there are those who develop a dependency; these are the ones that need immediate intervention and help learning to make better decisions.

It is impossible to predict which teens will experiment and stop and which ones will develop serious problems. Know what your teen is doing and who they are doing it with. The following are some warning signs of teenagers at risk for developing serious prescription drug dependency:
- A family history of substance or alcohol abuse
- Depression
- Low self-esteem
- Feel like they don't fit in and are not popular with the mainstream

- Frequently feel sluggish and have difficulty sleeping
- Aggressive and rebellious attitude toward authority figures

Prescription drug abuse is increasing; the main reason is that they are so easily accessible. If your child has one or more of the above behaviors, seek help from a professional.

Some things that you can share with your teen about prescription medications are:

- pharmaceuticals taken without a prescription or a doctor's supervision can be just as dangerous as taking illicit drugs or using alcohol
- Abusing painkillers is like abusing heroin because their ingredients are similar (both are opiates).
- Prescription medications are powerful substances. Medications help sick people and are administered by a doctor. When prescription medication is not used for sickness and not administered by a professional, it becomes an illegal substance and the impact on the person can be deadly.
- Many pills look the same and teenagers may get them mixed up. This can cause different reactions in different people due to the body's chemistry. It is extremely dangerous to take pills that are unknown.
- Mixing drugs with other substances is very dangerous. Some people have allergic reactions to different chemicals when they are mixed together.

What can you do to help prevent teens or any other person from getting involved with prescription drug abuse? The best thing to do is keep your prescription drugs in a safe place. Don't put them in the medicine cabinet in your bathroom because that is the first place teenager's will look. If possible, lock them up in a cabinet or safe box. Talk to your teen and warn them of the dangers of prescription drug abuse.

Avoiding Dating Violence

Whether your teen has known her boyfriend or date for seven years or seven days, she should be conscious of the person's behavior at all times and not put her safety at risk. Pass along these warning signs to your children so that they can respond proactively to a threatening situation rather than reactively. If your date exhibits these behaviors, he/she is probably someone you should not date.

- Acts jealous and possessive.
- Won't let you have friends.
- Checks up on you.
- Refuses to accept breaking up.
- Bosses you around.
- Insists on making all decisions.
- Belittles you and your opinions.
- Frightens or threatens you.
- Owns, uses or talks a lot about weapons.
- Acts violent, getting into fights or angering quickly.
- Pushes, grabs, pinches or hits you.
- Pressures you for sex or gets serious about your relationship too fast.
- Uses alcohol or other drugs and pressures you to do the same.
- Threatens to hurt himself or herself to make you comply with their demands.
- Demands that you lie to others about your relationship with him.
- Has been involved in a number of failed relationships.

What can your child do to protect herself in a threatening situation?
Here's some advice you can provide to him or her:

- Talk to someone you trust and can help, like a parent, friend, counselor or clergyman.
- Tell a school counselor or security officer what's going on.
- Make daily notes about the disturbing behavior.
- Avoid being alone with your date at home, school, work or anywhere else.
- When you go out, tell someone where you are going, who you are with and when you'll be back.
- Plan and rehearse what you will do if your date gets abusive.

If a friend of yours is a victim of dating violence, here are some ways you can help:

- If you see signs of abuse, talk to your friend about it.
- Tell your friend that you're worried and want to help.
- An abusive partner often undermines the victim's self-confidence, so point out your friend's good qualities.
- Encourage your friend to talk to a trusted adult, offering to go along.
- If the situation is getting worse, talk to an adult yourself, and if you witness an assault, contact the police, school principal or other adult immediately.
- Don't endanger yourself by confronting the abusive partner.

Things To Remember For A Safe Spring Break:

Top 10 Spring Break Tips include:

1. Get to know your surroundings before you go out and learn a well-lit route back to your hotel or rental property.
2. Always carry emergency cash and keep phone numbers for local cab companies handy.
3. Form a buddy system with close friends and agree on a secret "butt in" signal for uncomfortable situations.
4. Trust your instincts. If you feel unsafe in any situation, go with your gut.
5. Avoid being alone or isolated with someone you don't know and trust.
6. Don't accept drinks from people you don't know or trust.
7. Never leave your drink unattended, and if you do lose sight of it, get a new one.
8. Always watch your drink being prepared.
9. Try to buy drinks in bottles, which are harder to tamper with than cups or glasses.
10. Avoid putting music headphones in both ears so that you can be more aware of your surroundings, especially if you are walking alone.

Sexual assault is a crime of motive and opportunity.

Unfortunately, there is no surefire way to prevent an attack. If you or someone you know is a victim of sexual assault, please know that the assault is not your fault and that you are not alone. Help is available 24/7 through the National Sexual Assault Hotline at 800.656.HOPE.

Notes

5 IMPORTANT THINGS I LEARNED FROM THIS SECTION:

1. _____

2. _____

3. _____

4. _____

5. _____

IMMEDIATE ACTION STEPS THAT I WILL TAKE TODAY!:

_____

_____

_____

_____

_____

_____

_____

_____

_____

_____

_____

_____

PART III

Protecting Your Home

How to Make Your Home A Less Desirable Target

There are few things more violating than coming home and discovering your door has been kicked in and your personal belongings ransacked. The sick, throat clenching terror when you look at the empty spot where your car had been parked or the incredible anger and outrage to see a window smashed and your property stolen.

The truth is that property crimes make up an overwhelming majority of all crimes. Homes, garages, cars and businesses are all equally susceptible to the attention of thieves. And these crimes frequently happen when you aren't there. Your absence is a critical component in planning for any security. It must stand alone against an all out siege.

To make your home as safe as possible, you need to take a "layered" approach to prevention. If one layer doesn't stop the criminal, then the next one will. That is because most honest people will look at a lock and see a barrier, a criminal on the other hand will look at a lock and see something that he has to get around. Despite the fact that burglars may not generally use violence on people, doesn't mean they aren't willing to use whatever force is necessary to get what they want. And that means they don't care how much damage they cause getting to the inside of your home. It makes perfect sense to them to bypass a lock by kicking in the door or smashing a car window to get to something.

There is no such thing as a home that is burglar proof. Yet, you can implement measures to try to keep the burglar from choosing your house as a target.

There are two simple words to describe what you need

to do to create a Safety Perimeter around your house, your family and your life - ***Target Harden***. Target hardening is a term often used to refer to physical security measures in a home or business. It is about taking steps to making your home or business (the target) as uninviting as possible to a potential burglar. The reality is that most criminals are opportunists. They are seeking easy targets. Therefore, taking appropriate measures to harden the target means the burglar will have to work far too hard to break in. It also means there is a significantly increased likelihood of detection and apprehension.

Their goal is to conduct their business undetected and to avoid apprehension. Therefore, the harder the target is to breach or obtain, the more likely they will move on to another. What are some of the things you can do to make your home less appealing to a burglar?

One exercise that will help is to walk out of your home and "think like the enemy". Pretend you've locked yourself out and there's no spare key. How would you get in? If you can find ways, so can a burglar! This exercise is about preparation, not paranoia. The best way to stay safe at home is to keep criminals out. Much of the advice about staying safe at home may sound obvious, but don't overlook it – a little bit of common sense can go a long way in preventing crime.

Strategies for shoring up the weaknesses around your home include:

- Make sure exterior door hinges are on the inside rather than the exterior - where an intruder can remove the pins and pull the door out of the frame.
- If you have double-hung windows, bolt the upper and lower sashes together or insert a metal bar in the track to prevent opening.
- To secure sliding glass doors, add a bolt lock or use

a "charley bar" to block the door closed.

- Use bars to secure basement or garage doors and add bars to basement windows.
- Most home burglaries occur between 8 a.m. and 5 p.m., so get in the habit of locking all doors and windows whenever you go out.
- Even if you are home (maybe out back gardening), keep the doors you can't monitor locked
- Don't leave ladders outside so criminals can have easy access to second story windows
- Invest in high-quality, name-brand deadbolt locks for all exterior doors.
- If you have a double-cylinder deadbolt that is operated by a key both inside and out, keep the key near the door so every family member can find it and exit quickly in case of fire.
- Alarm systems are an effective deterrent. Nine out of ten convicted burglars agree they'd avoid a house protected by an alarm system.
- Security system decals and signs are also an effective deterrent.
- According to the FBI, more burglaries occur in July and August than in any other months.
- Make sure your security system includes a loud inside alarm, detectors at all exterior doors, and motion sensors in the master bedroom and main living areas.
- Never leave an answering machine message indicating you're not at home. Instead, just say you "can't come to the phone."
- Install motion-detecting outdoor floodlights around your home. Remember to mount them high enough to prevent intruders from disabling them.
- If there's a Neighborhood Watch Program in your community, join it. If there's not, start one.
- Report any suspicious persons or vehicles to your local police.

- Get to know your neighbors.
- If you have elderly or incapacitated friends or relatives, check to make sure their security devices are all in good working order.
- Some burglars scan newspapers for wedding and funeral announcements and special community and holiday events that might take you out of your home, so be especially careful on these occasions.
- Don't leave valuables in sight through windows, where they will tempt burglars.
- Use an etching pen to mark an ID number, like your driver's license number, on valuables.
- Make an inventory of valuables in your household and store it somewhere other than your home, such as in a safe deposit box.
- Leave curtains slightly parted so your house doesn't have an empty look.
- Prune overgrown trees and shrubs to eliminate hiding places for intruders.
- Many garage door openers respond to common codes, so follow the manufacturer's instructions to program yours with a unique code no burglar's opener will match.
- Don't leave your garage door opener visible in your car if it's parked outside. Many criminals break car windows and steal the openers to gain entry into homes.
- Keep your inner garage door locked at all times, preferably with a deadbolt lock.
- Thieves always look in mailboxes, under doormats and above doorways for keys. Don't make it easy for them to get into your home.
- Don't put your name or address on your key ring, because it might lead a thief right to your door with key in hand.
- When having a car parked or serviced, leave only

the car keys, taking your house keys with you — burglars can "borrow" such keys long enough to copy them!

- If there's any chance a previous resident may still have keys to your house, re-key the locks. Do the same if you lose your key chain or have any reason to suspect that a key to your house could be in the wrong hands.

Just as we advise our children "Never Talk to Strangers", NEVER open your door to a stranger. No one intentionally puts out a welcome mat to a criminal, yet unsuspecting victims open their doors to intruders all the time, often without even thinking to ask, "Who's there?"

The simplest way to protect yourself at the front door is to observe the person on the other side before opening the door — preferably without being seen yourself. Ideally you would do this through a peephole. If you do not know the person, you can either ignore them altogether or speak through the door (or intercom), to find out whom they are and what they want. Trust your instincts. You do not have to be overly paranoid, but if you are at all suspicious, do not open the door. As long as your door is closed, you have a relative degree of safety. Once you open the door, however, anything can happen. And do not rely on a door chain for protection if you plan on partially opening the door. Chains are notoriously ineffective and easy to break if someone wants to enter your house.

Here's how to handle different types of people at your door.

Emergency calls. Suppose two people came to your door saying they just had a terrible accident and need to use your phone right away. What would you do? Stop first, and think. You are home alone and something does not feel right about the situation. Trust your instincts. Do not let the couple in. Instead, offer to call the emergency number so they can return to the scene and wait for help to arrive. Some con artists have been known to use the emergency ruse to get into homes and commit robberies.

Fundraisers and solicitors. If a person comes to your door asking for money for a cause or wanting to sell you a product, and you're not interested in the cause or product, simply say so. If you are interested, either ask them to show identification first, before you open the door, or request that they leave literature for you to read. You could also ask the person to return later; specify a time when you know you will not be alone. Should the solicitor become rude, ask them to leave, and then walk away from the door. If they don't leave, call the police.

Repairs, deliveries and collections. Unless you are expecting them, ask repair people and others who claim to have business with you to hold up their identification cards for you to see through a peephole or door window. If you have the slightest doubt of their authenticity, telephone their business office (get the number from the phone book or from information) to verify whether the house call is legitimate. Do the same with individuals making deliveries or taking collections. If you are not expecting a floral arrangement, you can call the florist to clear up any doubts about the person making the delivery. If someone claims to be collecting for your newspaper subscription, and it is not the usual person, do not open your door. Instead, call the newspaper office and let them know you will be mailing in a check, or wait until your regular delivery person is back on the job.

Do not leave repair people alone in your home unless you know them well. And if you have any suspicions about them, do not stay in the house alone with them.

Keep mace / pepper spray by the front door in case of an emergency.

Apartment Living

Does your-

- Entry door have a deadbolt lock and peephole?
- Sliding glass door have a wooden rod in the track so it can't be opened and pins in the overhead frame so it can't be lifted out?
- Landlord or building manager tightly control all keys?

For extra security, leave a radio playing or a light on while you are gone. Always tell neighbors and the building manager when you leave for a business trip or vacation.

Check Out Your Building

- Is there some kind of control over who enters and leaves the building?
- Are walkways, entrances, parking areas, elevators, hallways, stairways, laundry rooms and storage areas well-lighted, 24 hours a day?
- Are mailboxes in a well-traveled, well-lighted area and do they have good locks?
- Are things well-maintained, are burnt out lights replaced in a timely manner, shrubs trimmed, trash and snow removed?

Check Out the Neighbors

- Get to know your neighbors. Join or organize an Apartment Watch group so neighbors can look out for and help each other.
- If you live in a large building or complex, think about a tenant patrol that watches for crime around

the building, provides escort services for the elderly and handicapped and monitors comings and goings in the lobby.

- Work with landlords to sponsor social events for tenants, a Sunday breakfast, a picnic, a Halloween party.
- Look beyond problems to root causes-does your building need a better playground, a social evening for teens, a tenant association, new landscaping, a basketball hoop? Work with the landlord for changes that make everyone proud of where they live.

Property Safety for While You Are On Vacation

Vacation time is supposed to be a fun time for the entire family. The last thing you want is to return home to find your residence has been burglarized. A few simple steps can help keep your home and property secure while you are away.

We DO NOT recommend that you cancel deliveries such as mail and newspapers. The fewer people who know you are on vacation, the safer your home will be.

HAVE A TRUSTED FRIEND, RELATIVE OR NEIGHBOR...

- Pick up mail, newspapers and any advertisements left on the door daily.
- Have someone cut the grass, water plants, rake leaves, shovel snow and do other yard work, as needed, while you are away.
- If you're planning to go away, be careful whom you tell.

- When vacationing, leave a car in your driveway or arrange for a neighbor to keep a car there and move it around from time to time.
- To a burglar, empty trash can mean you're away. Keep some trash on hand, and consider asking a neighbor to set out trash for pick-up at your house.

STEPS TO TAKE BEFORE LEAVING...

- Install timers to turn lights, televisions and sound systems on and off at different times to give your home a "lived-in look" when you are away.
- Make sure outdoor lights are on dusk to dawn timers.
- Install motion detector lighting outside.
- If you have a burglar alarm, make sure it is set properly.

These tips are basic but important. The more your house appears occupied while you are on vacation, the less likely you are to become a burglary victim.

Plan to Be Safe – Questionnaire

You might want to use the following information as a guide when you check your home for safety measures. The No's you've circled are areas where you can take action to improve your home's security. These are just some of the steps you can take to decrease the likelihood that you or your home is targeted.

Exterior Doors

- All doors are locked at night and every time we

leave the house, even if it's just for a few minutes.
YES/NO

- Doors are solid hardwood or metal clad. **YES/NO**

- Doors feature wide-angle peepholes at heights
everyone can use. **YES/NO**

- If there are glass panels in or near our doors, they
are reinforced in some way so that they cannot be
shattered. **YES/NO**

- All entryways have a working, keyed entry lock and
sturdy deadbolt lock installed into the frame of the
door. **YES/NO**

- Spare keys are kept with a trusted neighbor, not
under a doormat or planter, on a ledge, or in the
mailbox. **YES/NO**

Garage and Sliding Door Security

- The door leading from the attached garage to the
house is solid wood or metal-clad and protected
with a quality keyed door lock and deadbolt.
YES/NO

- The overhead garage door has a lock, which is used,
so that we do not rely solely on the automatic door
opener to provide security. **YES/NO**

- The sliding glass door has strong, working key
locks. **YES/NO**

- A dowel or a pin to secure a glass door has been

installed to prevent the door from being shoved aside or lifted off of the tracks. **YES/NO**

- The sliding glass door is locked every night and each time we leave the house. **YES/NO**

Protecting Windows

- Every window in the house has a working lock or is securely pinned. **YES/NO**

- Windows are always locked, even when they are opened a few inches for ventilation. **YES/NO**

Outdoor Security

- Shrubs and bushes are trimmed so there is no place for someone to hide. **YES/NO**

- There are no dark areas around our house, garage or yard at night that would hide a prowler. **YES/NO**

- Every outside door has a bright, working light to illuminate visitors. **YES/NO**

- Floodlights are used appropriately to ensure effective illumination. **YES/NO**

- Outdoor lights are on in the evening, whether someone is at home or not or a photocell or motion-sensitive lighting system has been installed. **YES/NO**

- Our house number is clearly displayed so police and other emergency vehicles can find the house quickly. **YES/NO**

Security When Away From Home

- At least two light timers have been set to turn the lights on and off in a logical sequence, when we are away from home for an extended period of time. **YES/NO**

- The motion detector or other alarm system (if we have one) has been activated when we leave home. **YES/NO**

- Arrangements are made for a neighbor/friend to pick up mail, deliveries and advertisements when we go away from home for a period of time. **YES/NO**

- A neighbor has been asked to tend the yard and watch our home when we are away. **YES/NO**

Outdoor Valuable and Personal Property

- Gate latches, garage doors and shed doors are all locked with quality, laminated padlocks. **YES/NO**

- Gate latches, garage doors and shed doors are locked after every use. **YES/NO**

- Grills, lawn mowers and other valuables are stored in a locked garage or shed, or if left outside they are hidden from view with a tarp and securely locked to a stationary point. **YES/NO**

- Every bicycle is secured with a U-bar lock or

quality padlock and chain. **YES/NO**

- Bikes are always locked, even if we leave them for just a minute. **YES/NO**

- Firearms are stored unloaded in a locker or safe and/or secured with a lock which renders them inoperable and ammunition is stored in a separate location. **YES/NO**

- Valuable items, such as televisions, stereos and computers have been inscribed with an identifying number approved by local police. **YES/NO**

- Our home inventory is up-to-date and includes pictures or video documentation. A complete copy is kept somewhere out of the house. **YES/NO** **How**

Auto Theft Prevention

What do you know about automobile theft? You may not know that most car thefts occur in residential areas, and that two-thirds of those crimes occur at night. Auto theft— specifically referred to as "motor vehicle theft" by the FBI — involves stealing the car itself. When someone steals the contents of the vehicle — the stereo, your CD's or the briefcase you left in the trunk — police generally refer to the act as larceny, or plain theft.

Almost any type of vehicle can be a target for thieves. Some vehicles are stolen so they can be used as getaway cars in the commission of other crimes. These thieves care more about a car's horsepower than its resale value.

Despite what you read about how easy it is for a

professional to enter a locked car, many times no real skill is needed. The sad truth is that more than half of stolen cars were left unlocked and the keys were left inside the vehicle in one-fifth of those.

Whether it's a youngster wanting to go for a joy ride or a professional thief wanting to resell your car to a "chop shop" that will dismantle your car and sell it for parts, thieves and carjackers are relentless and cunning. According to the FBI, an average of 1 of every 117 registered motor vehicles is stolen. In fact, a car is stolen every two minutes in the United States. Don't be one of those unlucky victims. *The best way to keep you, your car and belongings safe is to remove the opportunity.*

Following is a long list of suggestions to keep you safe. Choose the car security tips that make the most sense to you and *make it part of your routine to follow them*:

- **Lock up.** By simply locking all doors, trunks, hatches and camper shells, you're way ahead of the game.
- **When leaving your car, take valuable items with you or place them out of sight**. Packages, bags, sunglasses or even loose change can attract car thieves. Putting things in the trunk may deter the thief, but trunks are sometimes the target of indiscriminate thefts. Clear your car, trunk and glove compartment of any items that don't need to be there.
- **Park safely.** If possible, park in well-lit areas where it is difficult for someone to tamper with your car without being noticed.
- **Make a police report as soon as possible if your car is stolen.** Give police the license number, make, model, color and year of your car. Mention any special features. By acting quickly you increase the odds that police will recover your car.

As in all other types of robbery, auto robberies / carjacking, involve one or more criminals taking your car from you by force. The robber may or may not use a weapon. Carjacking can occur when you stop at a corner for a red light or when you go to a convenience store late at night. Carjackers, like other robbers, prefer to attack a person who is alone rather than with a carload of people.

Common sense and the practical tips in this section can help you avoid carjacking:

Be alert. Use your self-defense knowledge and tactics to protect yourself in and around your car. Have your keys out and ready to open the door. Visually scan the area around your car before approaching it. Pay attention to road conditions and stay alert as you drive. Do not daydream.

Lockup. Whenever you are in your car, keep your car doors locked and windows rolled up. This will help prevent an attacker from reaching into your car, opening the door and grabbing you.

Be careful where you park. If you stop at a pay phone or gas station, you should park in a well-lit area where you are visible to an attendant and other customers. If you park on the street, look around before you pull into your spot. Check to see if anyone suspicious is hanging around or if people are sitting in parked cars nearby. You can always drive around the block or find another parking space if you sense that something is not right.

Check inside and around your car. Before you get into your car, always glance into the back seat and down at the floors to see if someone is hiding there. If you often drive at night, keep a flashlight handy — perhaps on a key chain or in a coat pocket — to shine on your car before you get in. Also, glance underneath your car from a distance as you approach; carjackers have been known to hide under vehicles. Newer cars are equipped with a remote that allows you to unlock doors and turn on the lights in the car as you approach. This device can help you spot an unwanted guest in or near your car. Many remotes also have an emergency or "panic button" which initiates the alarm.

Don't fall for a "bump-and-run." Some carjackers use the tactic of hitting a car from behind at a relatively slow speed. When the driver of the impacted car gets out to asses the damage, the robbers steal the car. The best response to this situation will depend both on the circumstances and your own intuition. If you are in bumper-to-bumper traffic in broad daylight, and someone hits your car, you might decide it is safe to get out of your car because a robber wouldn't be able to go anywhere even if he tried. But if you are alone and it's late at night, you might stick your arm out the window and point to a nearby gas station, police station or some other well-lit public place and signal for the other driver to follow you there. When you get to a safer place, you can then exchange phone numbers for insurance purposes. Some drivers roll down their window an inch and wait for the driver who caused the accident to approach. By exchanging information through the crack in the window, you remain somewhat protected. Always contact the police to request that an officer respond to your location and inform the other driver that you have done so. Some car robbers swoop in front of a person's moving car and force them to slam on the brakes, causing a minor accident. Again, use your common sense and judgment and the self-protective tactics for the bump-and-run tactic mentioned above.

Although you're not supposed to leave the scene of an accident, if you feel you are in danger, keep driving. If circumstances or your intuition suggest that you are in danger, drive to the nearest police station or to a safe public area. Call the police to advise them of the situation and your location. Remember to always leave enough space between your vehicle and the vehicle in front of you to allow you easy egress when stopped at a traffic signal or stop sign.

Exercise caution if your car breaks down. When you have car trouble and someone stops to help you, you do not have to open your door or get out of your car. Rather, roll your window down just enough to speak to the person. Advise them that you have contacted the local police or highway patrol. If you have a "call police" sign place it visibly in your window.

Make a report — not a stop — if you see someone else with car trouble. It's best not to stop unless it's clearly safe to do so. Note the model and color of the car, as well as the license plate number and call the local police or highway patrol to report the problem. Even if you drive past an apparent accident, use caution. Staging fake accidents to lure unsuspecting victims has been used by criminals since the days of the Model-T.

Avoid confrontations with other drivers. Do not risk your life by arguing with another driver. Not only are cars lethal weapons, but you have no way of knowing if the other driver is armed. Tragedies have resulted from senseless arguments over turn signals and other minor issues. If another driver is rude or insulting, continue driving safely — don't let yourself be drawn into an altercation.

Don't let a suspicious car follow you home. If you are being followed, don't drive directly home. **First take the 4 right turn test**. If you feel someone is truly following you, make four right turns. No one should make these turns with you unless they are following you on purpose. Drive, instead, to the nearest police or fire station, hospital emergency entrance, all-night restaurant or other safe place. Call police to let them know your suspicions and, if possible, give a description of the driver and car.

Keep your garage or driveway secure. Install an automatic garage door opener and motion sensor lights at your home. When you pull into your driveway, the lights should go on and illuminate anyone lurking nearby. An automatic door opener could prevent someone from attacking you because you don't have to get out of your vehicle to open the garage door. Once in the garage, look around before you get out of your car, to make sure no one entered the garage after you. If your garage is not attached to your house, be sure the bushes are trimmed and no other obstructions block your view of the area between the spot where you park and your door or entryway.

Give up your car. If confronted by a robber, police advise that you do not resist or argue with the person, especially if the person is armed. Give up your car and get away.

Keep up good auto maintenance. If your car is well-maintained, it is less likely to break down on the road, which makes you less vulnerable to car-related crime. Keep your gas tank at least one quarter full. Make sure your tires (including spares) have the correct air pressure and are in good condition. Store an emergency kit with flares or emergency light, basic tools, a blanket, matches and an umbrella or rain poncho in the trunk. You may also want to invest in a portable device for repairing or inflating tires in an emergency.

Never allow yourself to be taken to a secondary location (kidnapped)! If you are abducted and transported to a secondary location your chances of survival are greatly diminished.

Summary Of Auto Safety Tips

- Always park in well-lighted areas, if you plan to arrive/leave after dark, don't park in isolated or visually obstructed areas near walls or heavy foliage
- Use valet parking or an attended garage, especially if you're a woman driving alone
- As you walk to your car be alert to suspicious

persons sitting in cars
- Ask for a security escort if you are alone at a shopping center
- Watch out for young males loitering in the area (handing out flyers, etc)
- If someone tries to approach, change direction or run to a busy store
- Follow your instincts if they tell you to walk/run away to a busy place
- As you approach your vehicle, look under, around, and inside your car
- If safe, open the door, enter quickly, and lock the doors
- Don't be a target by turning your back while loading packages into the car
- Make it your habit to always start your car and drive away immediately
- Teach and practice with your children to enter and exit the car quickly
- Drive with your car doors locked and windows rolled up
- When stopped in traffic, leave room to maneuver and escape, if necessary
- If you are bumped in traffic, by young males, be suspicious of the accident
- Wave to follow, and drive to a gas station or busy place before getting out
- If you are ever confronted by an armed carjacker don't resist unless they try to force you to go with them
- Never allow yourself to be taken to a secondary location. Drop the cars keys and run and scream for help to draw attention to yourself
- If you are forced to drive, consider crashing your car near a busy intersection so bystanders can come to your aid and call the police

- Call the police immediately to report the crime and provide detailed information
- Always have your keys in hand to unlock the door quick and easily.
- Never search for keys in your purse or bags while walking to your car.
- Never park in dark areas. Always park in well-lit areas.
- Always have a cell phone handy for emergencies.
- Never pick up hitchhikers.
- If you notice you're being followed, **DO NOT DRIVE HOME!** Drive to the nearest business, police department or fire department for help.
- Keep your vehicle in good working condition, to include tune-ups and tires.
- Always make sure you have enough fuel.
- Always have a map handy.
- Do not use cellular phones while driving
- Do not fix or apply makeup while driving.
- If you park your car outside of the garage at night, take your garage door opener inside with you.
- If in distress use your emergency lights or flashers.
- Always be courteous to other driver to avoid road rage.
- Do not go to rest stops at night alone.

Property Often Stolen From Vehicles

1. audio/visual equipment
2. cell phones
3. personal electronic devices
4. purses/wallets
5. sunglasses
6. checkbooks
7. cameras
8. spare change

9. compact discs
10. power/hand tools
11. briefcases
12. gym bags
13. auto parts/car batteries

What if Your Car is Stolen?

If in the event your car is stolen, there are measures you can take to help with its speedy and safe return:

- Report the theft to the police immediately. The sooner you report the theft; the sooner authorities can alert surrounding areas of your vehicle's information and description.
- There are devices on the market that allow police to track the exact location of an automobile, without the thief even knowing. Some of the aforementioned devices can even allow your vehicle to be remotely disabled. If your car has such a device be sure to advise the police.
- Carry a photocopy of your vehicles current license plate registration and insurance card, this will help you give the authorities the information they need quickly.
- Marking your car is a simple easy task to undertake. You can engrave your initials on the inside of the trunk or dashboard. This will help identify your car regardless of the condition in which it is found.

Notes

5 IMPORTANT THINGS I LEARNED FROM THIS SECTION:

1. _____

2. _____

3. _____

4. _____

5. _____

IMMEDIATE ACTION STEPS THAT I WILL TAKE TODAY!:

_____

_____

_____

_____

_____

_____

_____

_____

_____

_____

_____

_____

PART IV

Safety In Transitional Areas

While making your house safer is imperative, it is just as important to be knowledgeable and aware while away from home. Reducing your risk can be as simple as creating a safety plan and thinking through what you would do in dangerous situations. Always carry a cell phone with you and walk in a well-lit area with another person. Be aware of your surroundings and be observant: maintain eye contact with suspicious people, be confident, and always be ready. In the case that you are faced with a dangerous situation, "always trust your instincts." The idea here, like with your house and auto protection is to convince these criminals you are not a good target – causing them to pass you over.

Data shows that for violent crimes occurring away from home, half were within one mile and 75 % were within five miles of the victim's residences. This data indicates that defending oneself is not a matter of being prepared for possible confrontations in an unfamiliar part of town or in another city or state, but right in your neighborhood, even on the street where you live. As the U.S. Justice Department's Bureau of Justice Statistics reported, 'Of the victims of violent crime, 22 percent were involved in some form of leisure activity away from home at the time of their victimization; 23 percent said they were at home; and another 20 percent mentioned they were at work or traveling to or from work when the crime occurred.'

As I mentioned earlier, there are many myths and misconceptions circulating the internet about what to do in case of a personal attack. Just as we advise our children on safety issues, we should remember and PRACTICE them ourselves!

Some things sound "neat", like "if you are ever thrown into the trunk of your car, kick out the back tail lights and stick your arm out the hole and start waving like crazy. The driver won't see you, but everyone else will. This has saved lives".

This, unfortunately, is not necessarily true. You need leverage and space first of all. Go to your trunk right now and see for yourself. See if you were put in your trunk if you would be able to do this. Newer cars just don't allow for it. But, newer cars do have releases on the inside that you can use to open the trunk. *The important point here: getting in there in the first place is a very bad idea!*

Another myth is women are abducted from /attacked at the grocery store parking lot the most, office parking/garages second and public restrooms third. *Remember, there is no one place that most people are attacked. Don't allow yourself to have a false sense of security. Attacks can happen anywhere at any time. As with anything, there is a no "one size fits all" approach to crime prevention but all criminals and intentions are different.*

IT'S ALL ABOUT AWARENESS - the ability to observe the world around us is far more important than any physical self-defense skill. By properly using awareness skills, most people can completely avoid potentially violent situations before they happen. Awareness skills include internal awareness; external awareness, general observation skills, and common-sense strategies such as learning how to not look, act, or think like a victim.

Therefore, if we revisit the triangle of crime, what a criminal needs for an attack to occur is: ability, intent and most importantly Opportunity! We have control over the Opportunity! Try to remove it from the triangle to avoid a crime in the first place!

SHOPPING 101

- **NEVER PARK IN DARK AREAS.** Always park you vehicle in well-lit areas. Never park in dark areas. When parking in dark areas you are walking into unknown territory. A stranger could be waiting to strike.
- **ALWAYS BE AWARE OF YOUR SURROUNDINGS IN MALLS AND PARKING LOTS.** It is very important to pay attention to your surroundings. Always carry minimal cash and valuables with you and if possible wear less jewelry. Never leave your things unattended. Always keep your purse or wallet nearby and closed. When walking in the parking lot, pay attention to things that seem out of place. Never let your guard down. Keep keys and a chemical deterrent in hand in case someone approaches you trying to cause harm.
- **CHECK THE VEHICLE BEFORE GETTING IN.** Quickly check your vehicle before getting in. Look through the back and front windows; check underneath as you approach and look for any signs of forced entry such as a broken window. Always lock the doors immediately upon entry.
- **CARRY A CELLULAR PHONE FOR EMERGENCIES.** With today's technology you can make yourself a little safer. By carrying a cellular phone, you can call for help or assistance.
- **TAKE A SMALL PURSE OR POCKET BOOK** Criminals are always searching for a target. Targets are usually women with large handbags. When shopping always carry a small purse or pocket book closed to your body for security purposes.
- **NEVER OPEN WALLET OR PURSE IN**

PARKING LOT Opening wallets and purses in parking lots is very common, but dangerous. Always have your keys in hand so you won't have to search for them in your purse.

- **SHOP IN GROUPS** When shopping travel with a buddy or several friends. By doing this you'll significantly reduce the chance you'll be victimized
- **STORAGE SAFETY** People who carry lots of packages through out the mall become targets for robbery. From time to time store packages in the trunk of your vehicle for safe keeping. If you don't have a trunk, store packages underneath a blanket or clothing on the floor.
- **INFORM SOMEONE OF YOUR WHEREABOUTS** Informing someone of your whereabouts can help police fill in the blanks if you go missing. Police will have a good place to start their search and may significantly reduce the time it takes to find you. This could save your life, especially if you have been abducted or are in distress.

SAFETY AT ATMs

"I had just gotten off of work. I worked at a shopping mall and needed money. As I was leaving I drove through the ATM - it was 6pm. It had been a long day. I was relaxing, jamming to radio and not paying attention. I did see a man hanging around behind my car and thought it was out of the ordinary but I was close to a bus stop so I didn't really think twice about it. My windows were down, my car was unlocked. It was still daylight and there were a lot of people milling around the lot so I really didn't feel that I was in danger. I was so very wrong. Within seconds,

I had a gun shoved into my face with an angry man demanding my money and for me to drive. I was extremely low on gas. We drove to a nearby gas station. I knew that if I were taken to a secondary location my chances of survival were decreased so as soon as we stopped for gas, I jumped from the car with the gun to my head and I ran and screamed as loud as I could. The man ended up taking off with my car (my purse and identity inside) but I wasn't hurt – he has not been caught" – Anonymous

No matter what your surroundings, do not take the situation for granted. It is incredible this victim survived and she was brave enough to keep fighting and remove herself from the situation. Since self defense is about avoiding these situations in the first place, if she had thought through different scenarios before this event, it might have been prevented. First, windows should have been up, doors locked as soon as you enter your automobile (this should be right before you hook your seatbelt as a habit), radio should have been down so she could have heard what was going on around her as she waited for her money, and she should have heeded her "inner feelings" of concern when she first saw the man behind her car. Those feelings were telling her she might be in a threatening situation. We tell our children to "listen to their inner voice" but as adults we forget to do this. We are too busy, push the feelings off as paranoia, or we are afraid we might be perceived as being "rude" in a certain situations. TRUST THOSE INSTINCTS.

So what can you do to prevent this type of occurrence?

ALWAYS BE OBSERVANT

Watch out for suspicious persons, especially two or more people in a nearby vehicle. If you see someone who just appears to be "hanging" around the area leave at once. Visit ATM's during daylight hours if possible.

USE DRIVE-UP ATM'S

It is much safer to use a drive-up ATM machine, compared to walking up to one. Most ATM robberies occur between midnight and 6 a.m. Always keep all windows closed except the one you are using, and all doors locked when using a drive-up ATM machine. Keep your car running and your eyes open for suspicious behavior. Watch the front, sides, and rear areas of your surroundings; use your mirrors, if someone approaches your vehicle on foot, cancel the transaction and leave immediately. If you must use a walk up ATM machine at night take a friend, try not to go alone.

PROTECT YOUR ATM INFORMATION

Your ATM information is very important, if placed in the wrong hands your account could be wiped out. If you're using a walk-up ATM machine, stand where the person behind you can't see you putting your PIN (Personal Identification Number) into the machine. Never write your PIN on the back of the ATM card or on a piece of paper. If someone steals your purse or wallet they will have quick access to your bank account through an ATM. Never leave receipts at an ATM, they often contain information that could be useful for an unlawful individual. Last but not least, never give account or card information over the telephone.

LEAVE AT ONCE IF UNCOMFORTABLE

If you see something strange or out the ordinary leave at once. Don't stand at the ATM and count your money, take the money and count it later.

VERIFICATION

Always remember to keep your receipts to help verify any charges and activities at the end of the month.

CARRY A CELLULAR PHONE FOR EMERGENCIES

With today's technology you can make yourself a little

safer. By carrying a cellular phone you can call for help or assistance.

WORKPLACE SAFETY TIPS

Many people spend a good portion of their time at work. This means it's just as important to use crime prevention skills in the workplace as it is at home and in the neighborhood. Whether the place of business is corporate headquarters, a restaurant, a store, an auto repair shop, or a person's home, common-sense prevention skills can make the workday safer for everyone. Tips:

- Keep your purse, wallet, keys, or other valuables with you at all times or locked in a drawer or closet.
- Check the identity of any strangers who are in your office. If anyone makes you uncomfortable, inform security or management immediately.
- Don't stay late if you will be all alone in the office. Create a buddy system for walking to parking lots or public transportation after hours, or ask a security guard to escort you.
- Report any broken or flickering lights, dimly lit corridors, broken windows, and doors that don't lock properly.
- If you notice signs of potential violence in a fellow employee, report this to the appropriate person. Immediately report any incidents of sexual harassment.
- Know your company's emergency plan. If your company does not have such a plan, volunteer to help develop one.
- If the company does not supply an emergency kit, keep your own emergency supplies (first aid kit, flashlight, walking shoes, water bottle, nonperishable food, etc.) in a desk drawer or trunk

of your car
- If you work at home, in addition to making your home safe and secure, you should hang window treatments that obstruct the view into your office. You don't want to advertise your expensive office equipment.
- Review your insurance policy - almost all policies require an extra rider to cover a home office.
- Mark your equipment with identification numbers, and maintain an updated inventory list (with photos, if possible) in a home safe or a bank safe-deposit box. It's a good idea to keep backups of your work in a secure, separate location as well.
- Follow the same caution with deliveries and pickups that businesses do. Anyone making a delivery to your home office should be properly identified before you open the door. Do not let the person enter your home. If you own the company, take a hard look at the physical layout, employees, hiring practices, operating procedures, and special security risks. Assess the company's vulnerability to all kinds of crime, from burglary to embezzlement. Follow basic crime prevention principles, and work with local law enforcement to protect your business.

DAILY ROUTINES AND HABITS

- Do not take the same routes or go at the same time on your regular errands. If you take your children to school, change that route occasionally as well.
- If you jog or ride a bike, change up your pattern every couple days so criminals can't anticipate

where you will be at a certain time
- While running / biking, don't wear head phones blaring music in your ears. It may seem nice and relaxing but you can't hear what it going on around you. An attacker can take advantage of the situation and the element of surprise. In addition, you may not hear an auto approaching and can put yourself at risk in many ways from being hit to being kidnapped.
- Criminals watch for the lights to go off in the Master Bedroom at night. Keep a light on or keep it on a timer in another room so it appears as if someone is awake and moving around the house.
- ***Do not become complacent about personal security issues.***

What If I Practice Personal Awareness & Still Get Attacked?

What if someone tries to force me to go with them?

React immediately: If he abducts you in a parking lot and is taking you to an abandoned area, don't let him get you to that area. If you are moved to a secondary location, you are as good as "dead" a majority of the time.

If you are able: Scream and fight. Don't ever give up! Hopefully you will have a personal defense weapon with you such as chemical deterrents, keys in your hands to stab into soft areas such as the eyes, or at the very least a whistle that you can blow in case you are too frightened and can't scream.

What if they have a gun?

If the predator has a gun and you are not under his

control, always run!

Police officers only make 4 of 10 shots at a range of 3-9 feet. This is due to stress. The criminal will only hit you (a running target) 4 in 100 times. And even then, it most likely will not be a vital organ. Run! Nine out of 10 people who are shot survive.

What if he is chasing me down the street?

If you are walking alone in the dark and you find someone following or chasing you. You may choose to scream "FIRE!" and not "help." People may not want to get involved when they hear "help," but "fire" draws attention because people are nosy.

Most importantly run! If the shoes you are wearing aren't comfortable or easy to run in, kick them off.

If the aggressor is closing in on you (within ten feet), find an obstacle, such as a parked car, and run around it. If you get the obstacle between you and the aggressor you may have a chance to catch your breath, look for a good place to escape and continue to draw attention to yourself and the situation. Your last hope may be getting under the car. Once you are under a vehicle there are things to hold on to, and he will probably not be able to get you out, and will most likely not come under for you. At this point, SCREAM and KICK at him. If he has a weapon, you may reevaluate. Again, these are only guidelines and each situation will be different. Use your common sense.

Report the Incident to the Police as soon as possible!

Again, like with the children, while you are calm, practice looking at people for 10 seconds and test yourself on the recall of descriptive information. That way, when you are questioned, you will be able to report all the pertinent information to the police.

The most important features to remember are ones that cannot change quickly:

- Gender
- Skin Tone
- Size (height and weight)
- Hair texture

Police will also ask for these additional pieces of information:

- Glasses
- Hair length
- Age
- Clothing worn
- Identifying marks on body such as scars or tattoos
- For males, any facial hair

The Bottom Line:
You Must Be Able To Protect Yourself

Safety is something we can no longer take for granted. Comprehensive training begins with such basics as enhancing one's awareness of possible threats and acting proactively to decrease the chances of becoming a victim. Awareness is more than just looking around. It is a proactive mindset that involves educated observation and effective response.

The unfortunate truth is that in many cases of violence, there were warning signs and windows of opportunity where violence could have been averted. This is why it's important to learn what to look for and what preventive measures to take. However, violence, by its very nature, is unpredictable. Even when we educate ourselves to recognize potential threats, it is usually impossible to know when violence will strike.

In order to respond safely and effectively, you may want to receive training on basic physical techniques you can use to defend yourself and help others. You need to know what to expect and how to react. Anyone who has been involved in a physical altercation for the first time knows the actual experience is nothing like what they thought it would be. Regardless of the person's size or strength, one doesn't have to be helpless.

Many of us are concerned about our safety when we are out on the street. Obtaining unarmed self-defense skills is a necessary element of street survival. Unlike various self-defense devices that might not be available at crucial moment, unarmed self-defense techniques always work and can give you real confidence in your ability to succeed. Unarmed self-defense involves the use of "natural weapons" of your body, including the hands, elbows or knees - these are hard body surfaces that, when used correctly, can cause an attacker pain and damage and redirect their focus. Developing skills in the use of your personal weapons should enable you to successfully defend yourself when attacked. "Unarmed self-defense" involves various skills (mental and physical) used for survival - not only fighting techniques, but abilities to **evade** dangerous violent confrontations. In contrast to sport-oriented martial arts, the goal of self-defense should be survival and escape, not winning. Distracting the attacker and escaping should be your primary goal.

Controlling your emotions, evaluating the situation, judging whether to "fight or flee" and not allowing our verbals to make a commitment our body can't fulfill, are all important considerations.

Your most important weapon is your BRAIN!

Personal Weapons

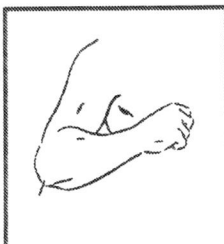

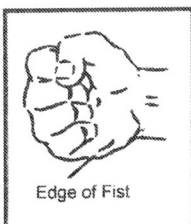

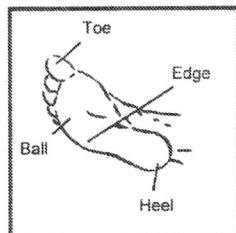

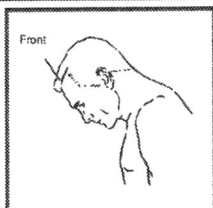

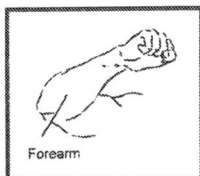

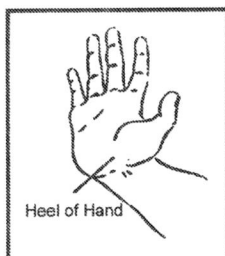

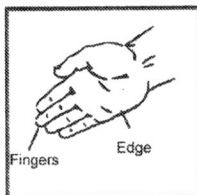

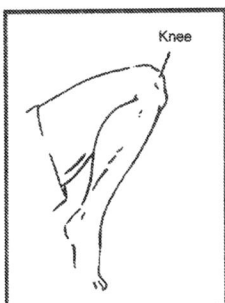

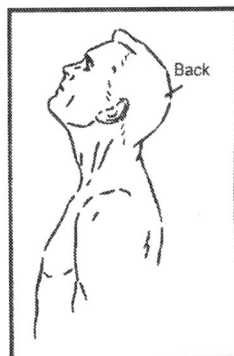

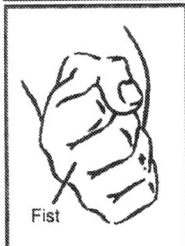

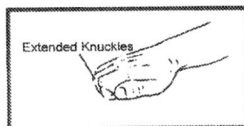

Edge of Fist

Toe

Edge

Ball

Heel

Front

Forearm

Heel of Hand

Fingers

Edge

Knee

Back

Fist

Extended Knuckles

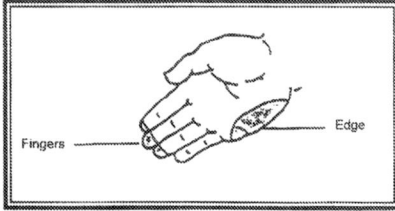

Fingers — Edge

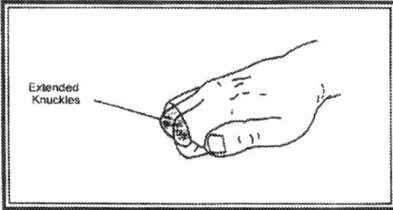

Extended Knuckles

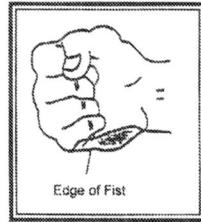

Edge of Fist

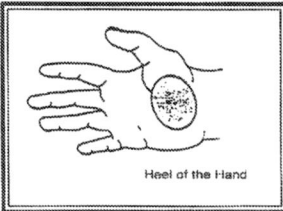

Heel of the Hand

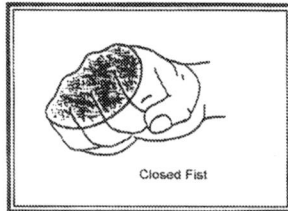

Closed Fist

VITAL AREAS TO STRIKE ON AN ATTACKER

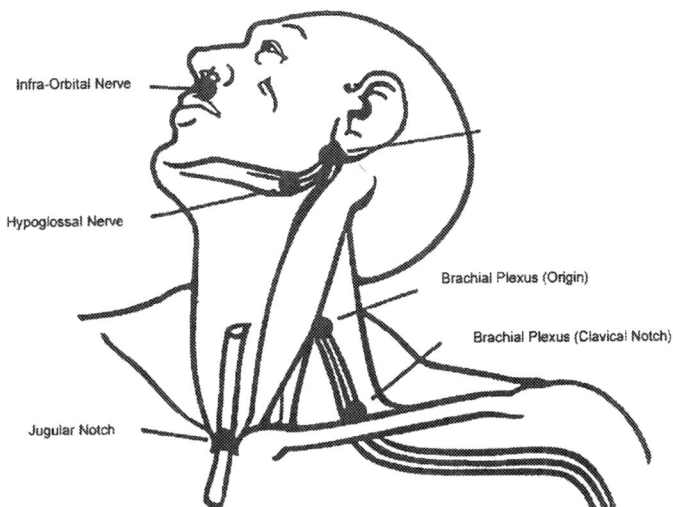

Infra-Orbital Nerve

Hypoglossal Nerve

Brachial Plexus (Origin)

Brachial Plexus (Clavical Notch)

Jugular Notch

Most everything we do in life begins and ends with balance. It is very important to maintain your balance before, during and after a physical confrontation. Keeping your balance will help keep you safe and give you greater mobility. By keeping your attacker off balance you can reduce their mobility and their ability to harm you. Your safety is once again enhanced.

The first thing you should do if you are physically attacked is to "drop" into a combat stance. A good combat stance is achieved by lowering your center of gravity by slightly bending your knees and taking a small step back with your strong foot (right foot if you are right handed) thus, placing yourself at a 45 degree angle to your attacker. Your feet should be about shoulder width apart and you should bring your hands up and prepare to block punches or grabs (think of the stance a boxer uses in the ring). When you move into the combat stance you also slightly increase the distance between you and the attacker. The following information is presented for the right-handed person, simply reverse if you are left-handed.

To advance from the combat stance, move the left foot forward and then bring up the right (Figure 1).

Figure 1

To retreat, move the right foot to the rear and then bring back the left (Figure 2).

Figure 2

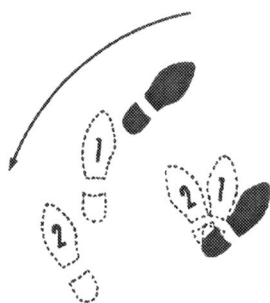

To circle to the left, move the left foot to the left as you pivot the right foot (Figure 3).

Figure 3

To circle to the right, pivot on the left foot as you move the right foot to the rear (Figure 4).

Figure 4

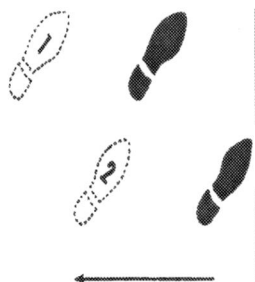

To move sideward to the left, move the left foot to the left and then move the right (Figure5).

Figure 5

To move sideward to the right, move the right foot to the right and then move the left (Figure 6).

Figure 6

FRONTAL CHOKE HOLD:

Rotate forward and strike with the heel of your hand to the area under the attacker's nose (infra-orbital nerve); follow through with a pushing and upward strike.

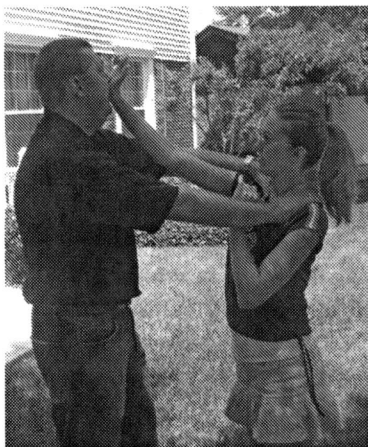

Blows to the nose as described and shown above are excruciatingly painful, invariably causing bleeding, impeding breathing and making the eyes water, thus causing vision difficulties. The nose and the infra-orbital nerve are particularly vulnerable to open-handed blows striking in an upward direction. If the nose is broken, breathing can become impaired.

The mouth is similarly vulnerable and the lips are prone to splitting and bleeding if a blow lands on a mouth unprotected by a gum-shield, but a punch in the mouth can also lead to injury to the hand if the fist comes into contact with the teeth.

Punching an attacker in the forehead or the back of the skull is likely to do as much damage to your own hand as to your assailant's head, perhaps even more. The head (as opposed to the face) is a particularly dangerous place to punch anyone and indeed one of the main reasons that boxers wear gloves is to protect their hands

This is about using your strengths against your attacker's weaknesses to REMOVE yourself from the situation – it is not about WINNING the fight. Most of the time, your attacker will be bigger and more powerful – so pitting strength against strength is only going to help your attacker win the fight. *This is not about fighting fair – this is about escape and survival!*

Other Options for a front choke hold are to:

Note: The throat can be attacked with striking techniques which cause a reflex gagging action as the person struck gasps for air. The extended knuckle strike is best for attacking this area, as the windpipe is protected on either side by the sternomastoid muscles of the neck. Be aware that the throat can also be an awkward target since experienced fighters keep their chin tucked low, which tends to protect this area very effectively. Quickly assess the situation you are in and use whatever means will work at the time and again, if one thing doesn't work, move to the next option – that is why practice is important – so you are familiar with and can utilize a variety of techniques.

1) Strike with your knuckles in the throat – follow through until the arm is completely extended.

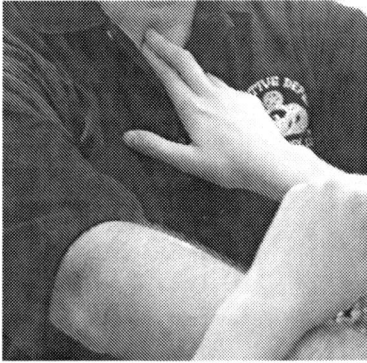

2) Place your middle finger over your index finger and jab inward and down as hard as you can, fully extending your arm and turning your shoulder into the push.

3) Connect your hands together in the center (one hand in a fist with the other wrapped over it) with one arm over and one arm under the assailant's as pictured below – "windmill" the lower arm up and the upper arm down while twisting away. This technique will give you a chance to escape, but the attacker can still pursue you.

4) Use a hammer fist to strike the collar bone as hard as possible. The bone is easy to break and will incapacitate that side of the attacker's body. Should you miss the collar bone there are several nerve bundles in the area which, when struck, can cause the attacker severe discomfort.

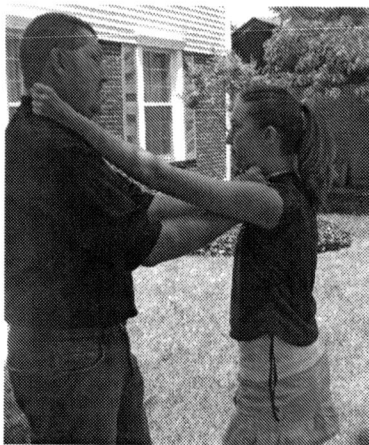

- For a child in this position, going for the shins, knees and groin are the places that will be the easiest areas to attack; for children, it may be hard to attack the face and neck areas with shorter arms than the attacker.

- For an adult, you have many options here because they have both hands occupied. You may also want to come down with both fists with all your might on the top of the forearm just in front of where the arm bends. Again, the object here is to get the assailant to release you. You don't want them to let go, turn your back on them and allow them to move in and grab you again from behind because now you have an upset perpetrator. Whatever you do make it worth while the first time, it may be your only opportunity to escape from the situation.

If an attacker grabs you by the collar:

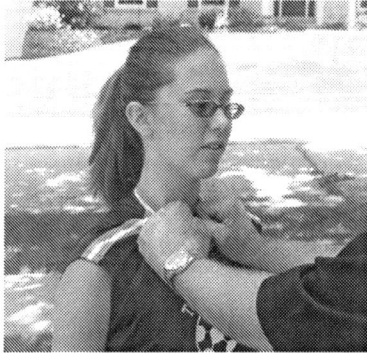

drop down lowering your center of gravity; and step back a little; this pulls your attacker off balance; with all your might strike up at the attacker's groin; or swiftly apply a sharp kick to the shin. If that doesn't work, do it again. You might also apply (as noted above) a strike to the windpipe, nose, forearms or collar bone.

If your attacker is in closer, use their body for support and balance and then apply your strikes.

If you have the ability and balance, you may also apply the heel of your palm to the nose as you strike with your leg, hit the collar bone or jab into the mandibular angle behind the ear and apply pressure forward.

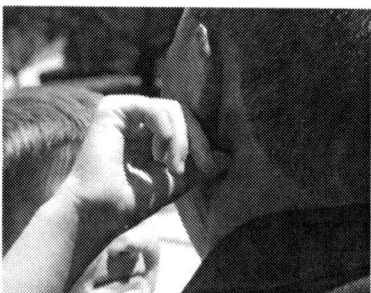

HAIR PULL

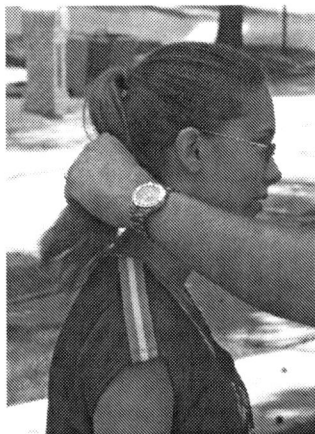

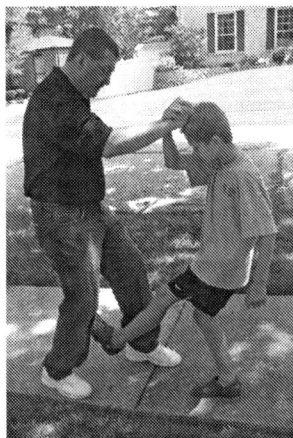

If an attacker should grab your hair, for women – your ponytail, you want to trap their hand tightly against your hand by wrapping your hand over the top of theirs. This way, their fingers can't get further entangled and they can't pull you around by your hair. "Where the head goes, the body follows".

At the same time, you want to drop slightly to lower to your center of gravity, strike and as soon as you feel their grip loosen pull away and escape. Kick or knee the groin, kick or scrape your shoe down the shins, stomp the top of the foot behind the toes near the ankle (these bones break easier and your attacker may have on steel toed boots so stomping on their toes won't make a difference). You want to hurt them before you move if you can, you want them to have second thoughts before coming after you. You want to get their attention away from you for a second so you can RUN and escape from the situation.

REAR CHOKE HOLD:

If your attacker has approached you from the rear and has you in a choke hold, you can place one hand over the wrist and the other near the back of the elbow. Turn your chin into the crease of the elbow to help you breath while dropping your body downward and pulling down on the arm to loosen the hold.

1. You can now choose to use the back of your head as a weapon and hit your attacker below the nose area.

2. You can use your foot to hit the assailant as hard as you can below the knee; continue using your foot to scrape down the shin and stomp on the top part of the foot as hard as you can.

REAR "BEAR HUG" GRAB

By grabbing a single finger and pulling it up, then back and downward to escape, you are employing the principle of forcing a joint through a range of movement for which it was not designed. This puts severe strain on muscles and especially on ligaments, which frequently tear when a joint is moved beyond the extremity of its normal range and so becomes dislocated.

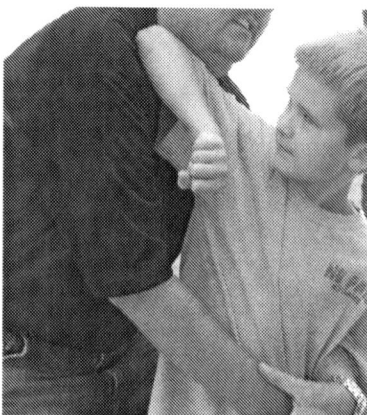

* Use of elbow to the throat or side of the head if grabbed

from behind

Again, use what ever weapons are at your disposal; an elbow to the ribs, a knee to the groin, shin scrape or foot stomp, grab a finger and bend it back until it snaps, the upper back of your head to their nose. These are all legitimate ways cause pain in order to escape such a grab. The idea is to stay on your feet and distract the attacker so you can escape.

If you should end up falling, try to remain on your back so you can continue fighting. Sit up on your elbows if possible and swivel on your butt. This way you can kick out at the attacker and deflect blows or attempts to re-gain control of you. At the moment you can regain footing, do so immediately.

Direct kicks to the knees, shins, groin or, if the attacker gets closer, kick into the solar plexus or face.

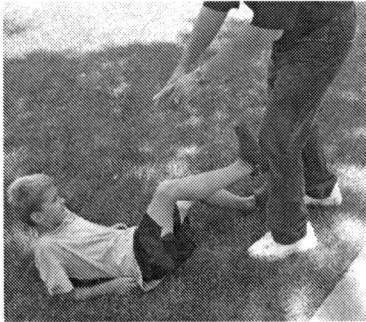

WRIST GRAB:

Open your hand and rotate your wrist toward their palm using a small circular motion, using the blade edge of your hand as a lever push down as you complete the circle. Using this technique will turn the attacker's body slightly away from you and should break their grip, but they are not hurt and may try to grab you again. Move away quickly, scream, put as much distance between you as possible, be prepared if the attacker continues the attack.

HEAD LOCK:

If you are in a head lock, slide one arm over the attacker's head and push up and back under the attackers head or nose (if they have long enough hair, grasp their hair and pull down and back) while placing your other hand behind their knee. Again, "where the head goes, the body will follow". Once they begin to fall backward the attacker will release their grip instinctively to break their fall. You may want to apply a kick to their ribs after the attacker hits the ground as a distraction to give you more time to escape.

OTHER AREAS OF VULNERABILITY:

The eyes remain a very vulnerable target and can be effectively attacked in order to distract an assailant and apply a throw or a locking technique. As the punishment should fit the crime, so the degree of force used should correspond to the seriousness of the threat an assailant offers. In the case of women, children or old people seriously threatened by an adult male attacker, aiming for the eyes may be the best chance for escape. If aiming for the eyes, use four open fingers slightly bent so as not to break them and strike into the eyes pushing in as hard as you can – then pull away and rake down the face. If you are a child and have a pencil or an adult with keys, you can effectively use those items as weapons against the eyes.

The solar plexus is another vulnerable area, being a large nerve group located just below the point of the sternum or breastbone. This is one of those areas that can be built up with training to be protected from assault, though.

As well as those target areas on the face mentioned earlier, there are places on the body that cannot be protected by any amount of weight training or conditioning, in particular the throat, kidneys and testicles.

The kidneys are located in the back just below the ribs and when struck cause a particularly sickening pain akin to that caused by a blow to the testicles. Obviously the attacker must have his back turned, or at least be side-on, in order for a strike there to be feasible, but this position can easily be achieved once any sort of punching attack is made. When an attacker is on the ground, perhaps after being thrown, he will frequently attempt to protect the front of his body by curling up in a ball, but in so doing he exposes his kidneys to serious injury from stomping kicks, the knee-drop or punches.

The testicles are probably the weakest point on any man and are susceptible to striking, kicking and squeezing attacks. They are generally indicated as the best target for a woman threatened by rape. Low kicks or knee strikes are effective when standing, as indeed is the low punch. When fighting on the ground it can be difficult to generate sufficient force for an effective strike, but grabbing, squeezing and twisting are very effective.

All of the aforementioned areas are very sensitive to pain and a hard blow should, at least temporarily, incapacitate most assailants to allow you a chance to escape..

NOTES

5 IMPORTANT THINGS I LEARNED FROM THIS SECTION:

1. _____

2. _____

3. _____

4. _____

5. _____

IMMEDIATE ACTION STEPS THAT I WILL TAKE TODAY!:

_____

_____

_____

_____

_____

_____

_____

_____

_____

_____

_____

PART V

What Travelers Need To Know

Plan To Be Safe

A female business executive, traveling with two male counterparts, arrived in London for an overnight stay at a four star hotel. The three checked in at the same time, chatting with each other at the front desk and making dinner plans for later that evening. They exchanged room numbers and agreed to meet at 9 p.m. that evening in the lobby. The three were unaware that many perpetrators hang around in hotel lobbies to gather information they can later use to commit crimes against the guests.

Shortly after the female executive arrived in her room, which as at the end of a hallway and across from the staircase – not a good location for a female traveler – she heard a knock on her door. She asked who it was, and heard someone say, "Lady, your associate asked me to bring you this package right away. He said you needed it for an upcoming report tomorrow."

The executive opened the door. Unfortunately, the person on the other side was not a delivery person working for the hotel, but an attacker who brutally raped her. Though she survived the incident physically, she was emotionally traumatized, suffering severe post traumatic stress that almost destroyed her life.

This case is just one example of how travelers are targeted by attackers. The tragedy is that the incident and many others could easily be avoided with a little advance training.

The executive's response to the stranger should have been, "Leave it on the front desk and I will pick it up later." She could have then phone her counterpart to verify the story and determined whether there really was a package. She also should have requested a less remote room when she checked in.

Criminals, intruders, stalkers, kidnappers and rapists worldwide profile us and chose to target people who are unaware, unfamiliar with their surroundings, and unlikely to fight back.

Safe travel doesn't just happen by chance. As with everything else in business and in life, preparation plays a big role in determining the outcome. The key to safe travel is to think about security from the start and to do your homework before you leave home. A good friend of mine was preparing for a trip to Hawaii. She knew the importance of safety and bought a money belt satisfied that her funds would be safe against her body for the trip. I had to laugh: "How are you going to feel safe getting out your money while pulling up your dress?" For she never wore jeans or slacks, her wardrobe only consisted of dresses. The point, what works for one person, won't necessarily work for another. The same is true for all aspects of personal safety. We need to all make our own individual check lists - planning ahead to be safe on a daily basis leaves you free of many unnecessary burdens and allows you more freedom to enjoy yourself, your life, and your travels free of violence.

Therefore, safety begins when you pack. To avoid being a target, dress conservatively. Don't wear expensive looking jewelry. A flashy wardrobe or one that is too casual can mark you as a tourist. As much as possible, avoid the appearance of affluence. Always try to travel light. You can move more quickly and will be more likely to have a free hand. You will also be less tired and less likely to set your luggage down, leaving it unattended.

Carry the minimum amount of valuables necessary for your trip and plan a place or places to conceal them. Your passport, cash and credit cards are most secure when locked in a hotel safe. When you have to carry them on your person, you may wish to conceal them in several places rather than putting them all in one wallet or pouch. Avoid handbags, fanny packs and outside pockets that are easy targets for thieves. Inside pockets and a sturdy shoulder bag with the strap worn across your chest are somewhat safer. One of the safest places to carry valuables is in a pouch or money belt worn under your clothing.

If you wear glasses, pack an extra pair. Bring them and any medicines you need in your carry-on luggage. Also have a copy of your passport and other travel documents with you and duplicates left with a trusted person at your home or office.

To avoid problems when passing through customs, keep medicines in their original, labeled containers. Bring copies of your prescriptions and the generic names for the drugs. If a medication is unusual or contains narcotics, carry a letter from your doctor attesting to your need to take the drug. If you have any doubt about the legality of carrying a certain drug into a country, consult the embassy or consulate in that country first.

Bring travelers checks and one or two major credit cards instead of lots of cash. Pack an extra set of passport photos along with a photocopy of your passport information page to make replacement of your passport easier in the event it is lost or stolen.

Put your name, address and telephone numbers inside and outside of each piece of luggage. Use covered luggage tags to avoid casual observation of your identity or nationality. If possible, lock your luggage.

What to Leave Behind

Don't bring anything you would hate to lose. Leave at home:

- valuable or expensive-looking jewelry

- irreplaceable family objects
- all unnecessary credit cards
- Social Security card, library cards, and similar items you may routinely carry in your wallet.

Leave a copy of your itinerary with family or friends at home in case they need to contact you in an emergency, again along with a copy of your passport and your immunization record.

Airport Safety

- Keep your eye on your bags—especially a laptop computer or other valuable gear — at all times. Don't let anyone but uniformed airline personnel handle or watch them.
- Be wary of mishaps, like someone bumping you or spilling a drink ... they may be staged to set you up for a robbery.
- Clutch your pocketbook close to your body or carry your wallet in an inside front pocket ... or wear a concealed money pouch.
- Record the contents of checked luggage and carry valuables onto the plane with you.

Don't draw attention to jewelry, cameras or other expensive items

Safety on the Street

- Use the same common sense traveling overseas that you would at home. Be especially cautious in or avoid areas where you are likely to be victimized. These include crowded subways, train stations, elevators, tourist sites, market places, festivals and marginal areas of cities.

- Don't use short cuts, narrow alleys or poorly-lit streets. Try not to travel alone at night.
- Avoid public demonstrations and other civil disturbances.
- Keep a low profile and avoid loud conversations or arguments. Do not discuss travel plans or other personal matters with strangers.
- Avoid scam artists. Beware of strangers who approach you, offering bargains or to be your guide.
- Beware of pickpockets. They often have an accomplice who will:
    - jostle you
    - ask you for directions or the time
    - point to something spilled on your clothing
    - distract you by creating a disturbance.
- A child or even a woman carrying a baby can be a pickpocket. Beware of groups of vagrant children who can create a distraction while picking your pocket.
- Wear the shoulder strap of your bag across your chest and walk with the bag away from the curb to avoid drive-by purse-snatchers.
- Try to seem purposeful when you move about. Even if you are lost, act as if you know where you are going. When possible, ask directions only from individuals in authority.
- If traveling out of the country, learn a few phrases in the local language so you can signal your need for help, the police, or a doctor. Make a note of emergency telephone numbers you may need: police, fire, your hotel, and the nearest U.S. embassy or consulate.
- If you are confronted, don't fight back. Give up your valuables. Your money and passport can be replaced, but you cannot.

Safety in Your Hotel

- Keep your hotel door locked at all times. Meet visitors in the lobby. Check the window in your hotel room to see that it is secure. This is especially true if your room is on the first or second floor or can be accessed from the roof
- Do not leave money and other valuables in your hotel room while you are out. Use the hotel safe if there is not one in your room.
- Let someone know where you are going and when you expect to return if you are out late at night.
- If you are alone, do not get on an elevator if there is a suspicious-looking person inside.
- Read the fire safety instructions in your hotel room. Know how to report a fire. Be sure you know the location of the nearest fire exit and where alternate exits are located. Count the doors between your room and the nearest exit. This could be a life saver if you have to crawl through a smoke-filled corridor.
- Don't leave your luggage unattended.
- Make sure your room has a peephole and deadbolt lock on the door and window locks ... and use them.
- Caution hotel personnel against saying your room number within earshot of others.
- In case of emergency, know where exits, elevators and public phones are located.
- If going out, ask hotel staff about neighborhood safety and areas to avoid.
- If someone claiming to be a hotel employee shows up at your door unexpectedly, don't let them in without first calling the front desk for confirmation.
- Don't display your room key or leave it where it may get stolen.
- **For illusion purposes, single female travelers**

may want to pack a pair of men's pants, and possibly a man's tie or shaving kit. These can be strewn around the room to give the housekeepers and others who enter the room the impression that a man in around.

- These items will also help when ordering room service – a situation that exposes female travelers to a degree of risk because they are letting a stranger – usually male – into the room. To make deliveries even less risky: with the "male items" evident, she should turn on the shower when the delivery person knocks at the door. She should have a pen in hand and a spot cleared for the waiter to place the food. As she opens the door, the woman should motion for the waiter to step in, while standing against the open door (this allows for an escape path if needed), she can motion for the waiter to set down the food, then for him to return and step outside, at which point she can sign the bill, tip heartily, and say goodbye, closing and locking the door behind him.
- While it is advisable to avoid direct confrontations whenever possible, travels should still learn some defensive maneuvers and if local laws allow, carry a nonlethal weapon, such as mace or pepper spray with them for extreme situations where no escape alternative exists.

Safety on Public Transportation

- **Taxis**. Only take taxis clearly identified with official markings. Beware of unmarked cabs or people who offer you a ride.
- **Trains**. Well organized, systematic robbery of passengers on trains along popular tourist routes is a

serious problem. It is more common at night and especially on overnight trains.

- If you see your way being blocked by a stranger and another person is very close to you from behind, move away. This can happen in the corridor of the train or on the platform or station.
- Do not accept food or drink from strangers. Criminals have been known to drug food or drink offered to passengers. Criminals may also spray sleeping gas in train compartments.
- Do not be afraid to alert authorities if you feel threatened in any way. Extra police are often assigned to ride trains on routes where crime is a serious problem.
- **Buses**. The same type of criminal activity found on trains can be found on public buses on popular tourist routes.

Safety When You Drive

- When you rent a car, don't go for the exotic; choose a type commonly available locally. Where possible, ask that markings that identify it as a rental car be removed. Make certain it is in good repair. If available, choose a car with universal door locks and power windows, features that give the driver better control of access to the car. An air conditioner, when available, is also a safety feature, allowing you to drive with windows closed. Thieves can and do snatch purses through open windows of moving cars.
- Study your route on a map before you start.
- Keep car doors locked at all times. Wear seat belts.
- As much as possible, avoid driving at night.
- Don't leave valuables in the car. If you must carry things with you, keep them out of sight locked in

the trunk.
- Don't park your car on the street overnight. If the hotel or municipality does not have a parking garage or other secure area, select a well-lit area.
- Never pick up hitchhikers.
- Don't get out of the car if there are suspicious looking individuals nearby. Drive away.
- Get to know the car you rented: Take a look at the dashboard (note the location of the speedometer, the temperature gauge, the gas gauge and so on). Locate the air conditioner, heater, windshield wiper and washer, defroster and light switches. Turn them on and off to make sure they work. Test the brakes to get the feel of them. Inspect content of trunk to make sure there is a spare tire and a jack in it. Check for any scratches or dents and report them to the rental agency before you leave the premises – you don't want to be held responsible for them when you return the car.
- In Case of Emergency – Be prepared to deal with a crash or other emergency situation while on the road. Review your insurance options with the clerk when you sign out the car. Know what your personal insurance will cover, and use that information to determine what additional coverage, if any, you may need to purchase. Be aware of the rental agency's emergency road service provisions. If they have no specific road service available, inquire as to whom you can contact in the event of an overheated engine, a tire blowout or a similar emergency situation.

Patterns of Crime Against Motorists

- In many places frequented by tourists, including areas of southern Europe, victimization of motorists has been refined to an art. Where it is a problem, U.S. embassies are aware of it and consular officers try to work with local authorities to warn the public about the dangers. In some locations, these efforts at public awareness have paid off, reducing the frequency of incidents. You may also wish to ask your rental car agency for advice on avoiding robbery while visiting tourist destinations.

- Carjackers and thieves operate at gas stations, parking lots, in city traffic and along the highway. Be suspicious of anyone who hails you or tries to get your attention when you are in or near your car.

- Criminals use ingenious ploys. They may pose as good Samaritans, offering help for tires that they claim are flat or that they have made flat. Or they may flag down a motorist, ask for assistance, and then steal the rescuer's luggage or car. Usually they work in groups, one person carrying on the pretense while the others rob you.

- Other criminals get your attention with abuse, either trying to drive you off the road, or causing an "accident" by rear-ending you or creating a "fender bender."

- In some urban areas, thieves don't waste time on ploys, they simply smash car windows at traffic lights, grab your valuables or your car and get away. In cities around the world, "defensive driving" has come to mean more than avoiding auto accidents; it means keeping an eye out for potentially criminal pedestrians, cyclists and scooter riders.

Special Tips For Senior Travelers

1. Did you know that Social Security MEDICARE doesn't provide for medical care outside of the United States?
2. Seniors constitute a large share of the travel market so be aware of VACATION SCAMS. Be skeptical about letters or postcards saying that you have won a FREE trip.
3. Never give out your credit card number unless you know the company
4. If anyone asks you to pay taxes on a "FREE PRIZE": hang up! It is illegal.
5. WALK with a purpose; don't look like you are sightseeing or lost. Be aware of who is around you including using eye contact
6. Carry all valuables – tickets, money, passports, etc… under your clothing in a body belt. Just keep what you might need for the day out of the belt.

In addition to personal safety issues, older travels need to consider their health before traveling. You're not as young as you used to be, but you're certainly wiser. You've reached a point in your life where you have the time and money to afford the kind of trips you've always wanted to take. But you're self-aware enough to realize that because of your age, you need to take certain precautions when traveling, especially if you're going overseas.

Preplanning

Prior to leaving for the airport, your first order of business is to thoroughly study your destination. Find out how the climate, elevation, water, and native diseases could affect your health. Determine what medical services are available, in case of an emergency. You should start planning your trip months in advance. This provides enough time to learn about the country you're visiting as well as to acquire the necessary passports, visas, and traveler's health insurance. Adequate travel insurance is important, especially of you have pre-existing medical conditions. You'll also need to determine what kinds of vaccines or boosters, if any, you may need. Even if you've been vaccinated for certain diseases, you may need a booster. Ask your travel agent if you will need any vaccinations. If you do, get your shots well before your trip, in case you suffer a reaction.

The Airport/Airline Experience

Prepare yourself for the airport experience. Busy airports can be confusing and frustrating environments. In the post-9/11 world, typical airport inconveniences -- such as long lines and long waits -- are magnified. Flight delays are always a possibility. When you couple that with a long flight, you may find that you are sitting for long periods of time. For the older traveler, this extended period of inactivity can lead to swollen ankles and clotted blood vessels. This can lead to a condition called pulmonary embolism, the blockage of an artery in the lung, which may cause permanent damage to the heart and lungs and even sudden death. To prevent this from happening to you, walk around as much as possible. Exercise your feet and legs while seated. Try to book a flight that has a stopover. If you suffer from angina or a lung condition, you may need to take oxygen, due to the high flight altitudes. Usually, airlines can arrange for you to have oxygen if you call in advance. You may also need to make some advance planning if you have other medical conditions, such as diabetes or urinary incontinence.

Special Supplies:

Use foresight when packing for your trip. Consider any health-related conditions and physical considerations. You may need to include:

- **Medications** -- Your medications may not be available in other countries. Supply yourself for emergencies and unexpected delays.
- **Medical Kit** -- If you're susceptible to relatively minor recurring health problems such as diarrhea and ear infections, pack a small medical kit filled with the necessary medicines. These items are not always readily available overseas.
- **Comfortable Shoes** -- When you reach your destination, you'll most likely do a great deal of sightseeing on foot. So, bring good walking shoes.

You've waited all your life to take a trip like this. Don't let illness ruin it for you. Take these preventive measures and enjoy the vacation of a lifetime – Safe Travels!

NOTES

5 IMPORTANT THINGS I LEARNED FROM THIS SECTION:

1. _____

2. _____

3. _____

4. _____

5. _____

IMMEDIATE ACTION STEPS THAT I WILL TAKE TODAY! :

_____

_____

_____

_____

_____

_____

_____

_____

_____

_____

PART VI

Special Safety Concerns
For Older Adults

Beware of Tricky People

Statistics show that the older you get, the less likely you are to be a victim of crime. But it still makes sense to take precautions, especially against *fraud and con games*, which are the greatest crime threats for seniors.

Safety Begins at Home

- Install and use good locks on doors and windows.
- Don't hide keys under the doormat, in the mailbox or in a planter. Leave an extra set with a neighbor.
- When service or delivery people come to your door, ask for ID, and check with their company if you're still not sure.
- Make sure the street number on your house is large, well-lighted and unobstructed so emergency personnel can find your home quickly.
- If you decide to install an alarm system, consider one that is monitored for burglary, fire and medical emergencies.

Stay Safe When You Go Out

- Go out with family or friends rather than by yourself.
- Hold your purse close or keep your wallet in an inside front pocket.
- Don't carry large amounts of cash or unneeded credit cards.

- Use a direct deposit service for Social Security and other regular checks.
- Keep car doors locked, be watchful in parking lots and garages, and try to park in well-lighted spots near entrances.
- Sit near the driver or the exit when riding on a bus, train or subway.
- If a person or situation makes you nervous, get away.

Don't Fall for Con Artists' Tricks

- If it sounds too good to be true – free vacation, miracle cure, sure-fire investment, driveway sealing, roof repairs – avoid it.
- It is illegal for telemarketers to ask for credit card, Social Security, phone card or bank account numbers to verify prizes, so if anyone asks, don't give it to them.
- If someone tries to rush you into signing an insurance policy, sales contract or anything else, be suspicious. Read it carefully and have a trusted friend check it, too.
- Don't buy from an unfamiliar company. Legitimate businesses understand that you want more information about them are and happy to comply.
- Always ask for and wait until you receive written material about any offer or charity. If you get brochures for costly investments, ask someone whose financial advice you trust to review them.
- Obtain a salesperson's name, business identity, telephone number, street address, mailing address, and business license number before you transact business. Some con artists give out false information. Verify the accuracy of these items.
- Before you give money to a charity or make an investment, find out what percentage of the money

is paid in commissions and what percentage actually goes to the charity or investment.

- Before you send money, ask yourself a simple question:"What guarantee do I really have that this solicitor will use my money in the manner we agreed upon?"
- You must not be asked to pay in advance for services. Pay services only after they are delivered.
- Always take your time making a decision.
- Never respond to an offer you don't understand thoroughly
- Never give out personal information such as credit card numbers and expiration dates, bank account numbers, dates of birth, or social security numbers to unfamiliar companies or unknown persons.
- Some con artists pose as representatives of companies or government agencies that, for a fee, recover money lost to fraudulent telemarketers. Don't fall for this trick.
- When in doubt, check it out by calling the police, the Better Business Bureau, the local consumer protection office, or the National Consumers League Fraud Information Center at 800-876-7060.

One of the most despicable crimes that is a growing concern, is the exploitation of the vulnerable, elderly. These individuals have saved all their lives so that they could stay at home and not live in a Nursing Home. Violent crimes against the elderly often make the biggest headlines. But abuse, neglect, financial exploitation and theft are what society's oldest generation fall victim to the most. These citizens are easy targets for victimization because they are so dependent on others for help. And despite numerous agencies and organizations, including law enforcement, which provides a myriad of services for the elderly, the problem continues to grow.

National Center on Elder Abuse estimates that 1 million to 2 million Americans age 65 or older have been injured, exploited or otherwise mistreated by someone on whom they depended for care or protection. With a range of definitions for abuse, there is no uniform reporting system from states or systematic collection of national data. It's hard to give the number any meaning, the National Center on Elder Abuse contends in its most recent published report, in 2005. Sadly, the crimes are committed by people the victim knows — sitters or family members.

One thing both national and local experts agree on is that exploitation and abuse of the aged happens more than anyone realizes.

Tips From Local Law Enforcement Agencies

- If you have a family member watching over your bank account, create a good rapport with your bank to watch for unusual transactions. Think about hiring a certified public accountant if it involves a large sum of money.
- Be cautious of those who come to the door looking for work, especially those who want to get paid up front.
- Once a year, get a copy of your credit report free from Equifax, Transunion and Experian.
- You can get a background check and credit reports on anyone through an independent company. There are many to be found online by doing a search for "background check."
- Acadian On Call system offered through the agency for $20 a month. The device is a pendant worn on a nylon cord. When the button is pushed, the system contacts the Acadian Ambulance dispatch that can talk with clients through the hands-free speaker and microphone box.

- Get to know your senior citizen neighbors. Set up a way to see if there is activity each day; for example, ask the elderly person to open a side curtain in the morning and close it at night.
- Do not open the door for strangers; use a peephole.

NOTES

5 IMPORTANT THINGS I LEARNED FROM THIS SECTION:

1. _____

2. _____

3. _____

4. _____

5. _____

IMMEDIATE ACTION STEPS THAT I WILL TAKE TODAY! :

_____

_____

_____

_____

_____

_____

_____

_____

_____

_____

_____

PART VII

Women's Issues

Domestic Violence

"I see invitations all the time to "tell your life or death story". I always wonder if mine is one of the stories people want to hear. He said, "You won't think it's funny when I take off your kneecap." He aimed carefully, like he had many times before, and pulled the trigger. I thought he had hit the entertainment center when the gun when off. After several minutes I realized he actually shot me. I didn't feel it. I saw it and sat down. I looked up and saw him standing over me with two guns pointed at me and his knife strapped to his side. I didn't get scared until he informed me that he was going to keep me, that he'd just swipe a prescription pad from work and write a 'scrip for antibiotics himself. He said he wasn't worried about anyone finding me because he'd just close the bedroom door and keep me tied to the bed. He said, "Don't forget, I'm an EMT, I can fix it so you go to sleep and bleed to death if you piss me off." For better than thirty minutes, I watched him act like something out of a bad made for TV movie, and reminded him how much I would bleed, how it was already staining the white carpet, how hard it would be to dispose of my body now that the neighbor (a construction superintendent)was through pouring concrete. I talked incessantly, but don't really remember what I said, just that I needed him to sober up. It was like God handed me an alibi for him and I began repeating it to him over and over and over until he dialed the ER and said, "This is David, and I just shot my girlfriend. I'm bringing her in; we'll need a wheelchair." All the way to the ER I kept repeating the story.

Occasionally he reminded me, "These people love me. They worked with me, they worship me. They'll tell me everything you say. No one will believe it was me. No one will miss you." - Anonymous

Domestic violence is a serious problem in America, with devastating consequences for individuals, families, and communities. Just as we must focus our efforts on securing the homeland against terrorist threats in the aftermath of 9/11, we must also find ways to protect our citizens from a different kind of terrorism – those acts of violence carried out in the "comfort" of a victim's home, by individuals with whom the victim has a close relationship.

Nearly 5.3 million incidents of intimate partner violence occur each year among U.S. women ages 18 and older, and 3.2 million incidents occur among men, according to the CDC National Center for Injury Prevention and Control. These incidents result in nearly 2 million injuries and 1,300 deaths nationwide every year. Violence against men by women and same-sex partners are also problems, although women report significantly more past and present nonphysical violence than men.

- More than three-fourths (76 percent) of intimate partner violence homicide victims were female in 2002. Although the number of intimate partner homicides decreased 14 percent overall in the span of about 20 years, the decline was much sharper for men (67 percent decrease) than for women (25 percent decrease).
- Research shows nearly half (44 percent) of women murdered by their intimate partner had visited an emergency department within two years of the homicide.
- Intimate partner violence costs exceed $8.3 billion. Victims of severe intimate partner violence lose

nearly eight million days of paid work, the
equivalent of more than 32,000 full-time jobs, and
almost 5.6 million days of household productivity
each year.

He says he's sorry and that it won't happen again. But
you fear it will. Angry outbursts, hurtful words, sometimes
a slap or a punch. You may start to doubt your own
judgment, or wonder whether you're going crazy. Maybe
you think you've imagined the whole thing. But you
haven't. Domestic violence can and does happen to people
of all ages, races, and socioeconomic and educational
backgrounds. Domestic violence happens to men and to
same-sex partners, but most often domestic violence
involves men abusing their female partners.

Domestic violence takes many forms, including
coercion, threats, intimidation, isolation, and emotional,
sexual and physical abuse. An abusive relationship is about
power and control.

Without help, abuse will continue and could worsen.
Many resources are available to help you understand your
options and to support you. No one deserves to be abused.
Though there are no typical victims of domestic violence,
abusive relationships do share similar characteristics. In all
cases, the abuser aims to exert power and control over his
partner.

In an abusive relationship, the abuser may use varying
tactics to gain power and control, including:

- **Children as pawns.** Accuses you of bad parenting,
  threatens to take the children away, uses the
  children to relay messages, or threatens to report
  you to children's protective services.
- **Coercion and threats.** Threatens to hurt other
  family members, pets, children or self.
- **Denial and blame.** Denies that the abuse occurs and

shifts responsibility for the abusive behavior onto you. This may leave you confused and unsure of yourself or make you feel like you're going crazy.

- **Economic abuse.** Controls finances, refuses to share money, makes you account for money spent and doesn't want you to work outside the home. The abuser may also try to sabotage your work performance by forcing you to miss work or by calling you frequently at work.
- **Emotional abuse.** Uses put-downs, insults, criticism or name-calling to make you feel bad about yourself.
- **Intimidation.** Uses certain looks, actions or gestures to instill fear. The abuser may break things, destroy property, abuse pets or display weapons.
- **Isolation.** Limits your contact with family and friends, requires you to get permission to leave the house, doesn't allow you to work or attend school, and controls your activities and social events. The abuser may ask where you've been, track your time and whereabouts, or check the odometer on your car.
- **Power.** Makes all major decisions, defines the roles in your relationship, is in charge of the home and social life, and treats you like a servant or possession.

It may not be easy to identify abuse. An abusive relationship can start subtly. The abuser may criticize your appearance or may be unreasonably jealous. Gradually, the abuse becomes more frequent, severe and potentially life-threatening. It's important to know that these relationships don't happen overnight. It's a gradual process — a slow disintegration of a person's sense of self. When you live in an environment of chaos, stress and fear, you start doubting yourself and your ability to take care of yourself. It can unravel your sense of reality and self-esteem.

Pregnancy is a particularly perilous time for an abused woman. Not only is your health at risk, but also the health of your unborn child. Abuse can begin or may increase during pregnancy.

Very few people identify themselves as abusers or victims. They may remain silent about the issue because of the havoc that domestic violence has created in their workplace and family lives. Victims may be silent about the abuse because of embarrassment or shame, or for fear that their batterers will hurt them if they tell other people about the violence. Abusers may minimize their actions or blame the victims for provoking the violence. Both victims and abusers may characterize their experiences as family quarrels that "got out of control."

Think about the following questions to identify whether you or someone you know is a victim of domestic violence. If you or someone you know is being abused, develop a safety plan right away even if you do not intend to separate at this time.

Screening Questions

Domestic violence is not confined to "certain groups." Do not try to predict who is a batterer and who is a victim of domestic violence. Ask the following questions to determine whether domestic violence is occurring:

- Everyone argues or fights with their partner or spouse now and then. When you argue or fight at home, what happens? Do you ever change your behavior because you are afraid of the consequences of a fight?
- Do you feel that your partner or spouse treats you well? Is there anything that goes on at home that makes you feel afraid?
- Has your partner or spouse ever hurt or threatened

you or your children? Has your partner or spouse ever put their hands on you against your will? Has your partner or spouse ever forced you to do something you did not want to do? Does your partner or spouse criticize you or your children a lot?

- Has your partner or spouse ever tried to keep you from taking medication you needed or from seeking medical help? Does your partner refuse to let you sleep at night?

- Has your partner or spouse ever hurt your pets or destroyed your clothing, objects in your home, or something which you especially cared about? Does your partner or spouse throw or break objects in the home during arguments?

- Does your partner or spouse act jealously, for example, always calling you at work or home to check up on you? Is it hard for you to maintain relationships with your friends, relatives, neighbors, or co-workers because your partner or spouse disapproves of, argues with, or criticizes them? Does your partner or spouse accuse you unjustly of flirting with others or having affairs? Has your partner or spouse ever tried to keep you from leaving the house?

- Does your spouse or partner make it hard for you to find or keep a job or to go to school?

- Every family has their own way of handling finances. Does your partner or spouse withhold money from you when you need it? Do you know what your family's assets are? Do you know where important documents like bank books, check books, financial statements, birth certificates, and passports for you and members of your family are kept? If you wanted to see or use any of them, would your partner or spouse make it difficult for you to do so? Does your spouse or partner sometimes spend large sums of money and refuse to tell you why or what the money was spent on?

- Has your spouse or partner ever forced you to have sex or made you do things during sex that make you feel uncomfortable? Does your partner demand sex when you are sick, tired, or sleeping?
- Has your spouse or partner ever used or threatened to use a weapon against you? Are there guns in your home?
- Does your spouse or partner abuse drugs or alcohol? What happens?

Basic Warning Signs
Controlling behavior includes:

- Not letting you hang out with your friends
- Calling or paging you frequently to find out where you are, who you're with, and what you're doing
- Telling you what to wear
- Having to be with you all the time

Verbal and emotional abuse includes:

- Calling you names;
- Jealousy
- Belittling you (cutting you down)
- Threatening to hurt you, someone in your family, or themselves if you don't do what they want

Physical abuse includes:

- Shoving

- Punching
- Slapping
- Pinching
- Hitting
- Kicking
- Hair pulling
- Strangling

Sexual abuse includes:

- Unwanted touching and kissing
- Forcing you to have sex
- Not letting you use birth control
- Forcing you to do other sexual things

If you are at home & you are being threatened or attacked:

- *Stay* away from the kitchen (the abuser can find weapons, like knives, there)
- Stay away from bathrooms, closets or small spaces where the abuser can trap you
- Get to a room with a door or window to escape
- Get to a room with a phone to call for help; lock the abuser outside if you can
- Call 911 (or your local emergency number) right away for help; get the dispatcher's name
- Think about a neighbor or friend you can run to for help
- If a police officer comes, tell him/her what happened; get his/her name & badge number
- Get medical help if you are hurt
- Take pictures of bruises or injuries
- Call a domestic violence program or shelter (some

are listed here); ask them to help you make a safety plan

My name IS Anne. I am only 21 years old, and I am living in my own apartment in New Jersey, since I just moved out of my parents' house. I was engaged to Michael, but because of his violent nature, I called off my engagement and am continuing on with my life. I love my job in sales, which I've been at for about a year and a half. I really feel like my life is moving forward

I recently met a young attorney, Richard, at a friend's wedding and we've begun dating. He sent flowers to my office on Friday afternoon and my co-workers said I "lit up like a Christmas Tree". It's the first time I've ever gotten flowers from a guy. I'm looking forward to seeing Richard this weekend.

Early Saturday morning, I hear a knock at the back door of my apartment. Still groggy from sleep, I answer the door am and shot five times at close range by my ex-fiance, Michael.

As I lie dying on my kitchen floor, he walks over my body and into the next room and shoots and kills my new boyfriend, Richard.

My name WAS Anne.

Remember my name.

Don't let this happen to someone you care about. Approach them with your concerns. If some one declines to discuss domestic violence issues, consider whether the silence may be due to a fear of the batterer, or to cultural, race or gender issues which make it difficult to talk about such personal experiences. If you suspect that someone is a victim of domestic violence, say the following:

- o I am concerned about your safety.
- o You can talk to me about what is happening at home.
- o Domestic violence can harm your children.

- o Domestic violence is a crime.
- o I will help you find the legal and non-legal service referrals you need.

And then follow through and do what you can to safely get them out of the situation!

Leaving an abuser can be dangerous. You're the only person who knows the safest time to leave. Make sure you prepare a safety plan so that you can act quickly when the time is right. Consider taking these precautions:

- Arrange a safety signal with a neighbor as an alert to call the police if necessary.
- Prepare an emergency bag that includes items you'll need when you leave, such as extra clothes, important papers, money, extra keys and prescription medications.
- Know exactly where you'll go and how you'll get there, even if you have to leave in the middle of the night.
- Call a local women's shelter or the National Domestic Violence Hotline at (800) 799-7233 to find out about legal options and resources available to you, before you need them.
- If you have school-age children, notify the school authorities about custody arrangements, warn them about possible threats and advise the school on what information to keep confidential.
- As part of a safety plan, avoid making long-distance phone calls from home because the abuser could trace the calls to find out where you're going. And the abuser may be able to intercept your cell phone conversations using a scanner. Switch to a corded phone if you're relaying sensitive information.
- Also, be aware that the abuser may be able to monitor your Internet activities and access your e-mail account. Change your passwords, get a new e-

mail account or access a computer at a public library

If you consider leaving your abuser, other things to think about might include...

1. Two or more places you could go if you leave your home.
2. People who might help you if you left. Think about people who will keep a bag for you. Think about people who might lend you money. Make plans for your pets.
3. Keeping change for phone calls or getting a cell phone.
4. Opening a bank account or getting a credit card in your name.
5. Again, think about how you might leave. Try doing things that get you out of the house - taking out the trash, walking the family pet, or going to the store. Practice how you would leave.
6. How you could take your children with you safely? There are times when taking your children with you may put all of your lives in danger. You need to protect yourself to be able to protect your children.
7. Putting together a bag of things you use everyday. Hide it where it is easy for you to get.

ITEMS TO TAKE, IF POSSIBLE

- Children (if it is safe)
- Money
- Keys to car, house, work
- Extra clothes
- Medicine
- Important papers for you and your children
- Birth certificates

- Social security cards
- School and medical records
- Bankbooks, credit cards
- Driver's license
- Car registration
- Welfare identification
- Passports, green cards, work permits
- Lease/rental agreement
- Mortgage payment book, unpaid bills
- Insurance papers
- PPO, divorce papers, custody orders
- Address book
- Pictures, jewelry, things that mean a lot to you
- Items for your children (toys, blankets, etc.)

Think about reviewing your safety plan often.

If you have left your abuser, think about...

1. Your safety - you still need to.
2. Getting a cell phone. If you do not have one the police, your employer, or an anti abuse organization may be able to provide you with one.
3. Getting a Protective Order from the court. Keep a copy with you all the time. Give a copy to the police, people who take care of your children, their schools and your employer.
4. Changing the locks. Consider putting in stronger doors, smoke and carbon monoxide detectors, a security system and outside lights.
5. Telling friends and neighbors that your abuser no longer lives with you. Ask them to call the police if they see your abuser near your home or children.
6. Telling people who take care of your children the names of people who are allowed to pick them up. If you have a Protective Order protecting your children, give their teachers and babysitters a copy

of it.

7. Telling someone at work about what has happened. Ask that person to screen your calls. If you have a Protective Order that includes where you work, consider giving your boss a copy of it and a picture of the abuser. Think about and practice a safety plan for your workplace. This should include going to and from work. You may need to request a safer parking place at you place of employment.

8. Not using the same stores or businesses that you did when you were with your abuser.

9. Someone that you can call if you feel down. Call that person if you are thinking about going to a support group or workshop.

HOW TO MAKE YOURSELF SAFER AT WORK

- *Keep a copy of your court order at work*
- *Give a **picture of the abuser to security** and friends at work*
- ***Tell your supervisors** - see if they can make it harder for the abuser to find you*
- *Don't go to lunch alone*
- *Ask a **security guard** to walk you to your car or to the bus*
- *If the abuser calls you at work, **save voice mail** and save e-mail*
- *Your employer may be able to help you find community resources*

Rape / Sexual Assault

" Surviving a life and death situation changes you forever. I have a classic story. November 15th, 1985; I was sound asleep in my own apartment. I was awoken to a man, sitting on my chest, beating my face with his fists yelling, "you hurt my brother - now I am going to hurt you" I recall telling this stranger..."you have the wrong person" when he continued to beat on my head, I realized he did not care if he had the wrong person or not. He continued to beat on me. He held a pillow over my head suffocating me. He then raped me. Holding a knife to my face, and cut my face with one clean cut. He then told me if I moved he would kill me. He slowly climbed off of me. I moved the pillow, he said sternly "I said don't move" I waited about 30 seconds and jumped up, ran out side and started yelling.....I woke up the neighborhood, I saw the lights come on. No one came out. I ran down the hall to a neighbor I had said hello to on occasion. She would not open her door. The young man next door opened his door. I meet him, shaking, bleeding, and shaking a butcher knife at him - screaming call the police. He had me come into his apartment, I would not give him the knife. He called the police. He as well robbed me, stole my purse which had all my keys and identification in it, and all my jewelry. Since then, I have become a much more cautious person. I will not stay in a dark area, no matter where I am, I will leave. I always carry my keys in my pocket. I keep extra keys stashed around. I only have one ring worth any amount of money. I have identification besides what is in my purse. And I always, always look around the house when I come in alone. A funny thing, about 2 weeks prior, I had a creepy feeling that someone was looking in my kitchen window. Afraid, I just locked the window and forgot about it. I now pay attention to those "things" I get once in a while. God Bless all the rape survivors. For it is one hell of a journey back!" - Diane.

Violence against women has been reported in every corner of our country. It cuts across every age, race, religion and economic segment of our community. Every woman from an early age is conditioned to alter her life, thoughts and movements in order to compensate for verbal, emotional or physical assaults against her.

At the present time, 2007, one woman in four will be a victim of sexual assault in her lifetime (and it is still the most under reported crime - only 10 % of rape victims report their rape to the police). If rapes continue to increase at the 1990-1991 levels, it will soon be one woman out of three then one out of two. More than 60% of rapes are committed by a person known to the victim. On college campuses, 84% of the victims knew their attacker. In 14% of reported rapes, the attacker is a close friend, a member of the family or a close family friend. In more than 80% of reported rapes, the victim and the attacker are of the same race and socio-economic background. The youngest reported rape victim was 2 months old while the oldest was 99. Almost 90% of rapes involved threats of physical harm or the actual use of physical force.

There is no pattern to the crime. Sexual assault occurs in the home and in the workplace, at the mall and the corner store, in kindergartens and on college campuses; it happens in the morning, afternoon and evening, to the plain and the beautiful, to the young and the old. It is a crime that degrades its victims and violates the most basic rights of freedom. It can happen to any woman or child, any time, any place. A vulnerable target and the right opportunity are the only two elements a rapist needs. The element of surprise always works in the rapist's favor.

There are no guarantees when it comes to self-defense. However, proper training can increase your level of preparedness. The suggestions outlined here are designed to increase your odds against sexual attacks. The more you know about preventing rape, the better your chances are of never becoming a statistic.

- **Dress to Kill:** Clogs, high heels, and tight skirts are hard to run and fight in, while scarves and long necklaces are easy to grab. If possible, modify your fashion style or wear comfortable clothing when walking alone. You can always change into dress clothes later. Or, think through how you would fight in your dress clothes. Would you kick off your high heels or hike your skirt up around your hips to run or kick; would you use a high heel as a weapon?

- **Make Eye Contact**: .It may be your first instinct to lower your gaze as you walk to your destination, but looking straight into the face of potential assailants is the better option. Eye contact is important as such may scare off attackers because they fear you will be able to identify them.

- **Keep your Eyes and Ears Open and your Hands Free:** It is important to be alert to whom and what is around you. Talking on a cell phone or listening to headphones makes you a likely target as well as easy prey for a predator. The only reason you should be using your cell phone is notify a friend of your whereabouts or to call for help. Also, limit the number of bundles you have to carry by using a backpack or bag with a shoulder strap. This will ensure that your hands are free to defend. Be prepared to surrender your backpack or purse as opposed to becoming the victim of a violent assault.

- **Be Lazy:** Take the Elevator Over the Stairs. And when in the elevator, stand in front of the doors, and then if someone you feel uneasy about gets on with you, you can step off immediately.

- **Fight Your Inner Woman.** Experts say that women tend to be sympathetic — don't be! History has shown that serial killers and other criminals often play on the sympathies of unsuspecting women to lure them into dangerous situations. If someone asks for the time, directions, or help in or around their car, be as courteous as possible but keep moving, and definitely move away from the potential assailant. You can always assist the stranger by making a phone call to police from a safe location, or by finding others to go back and help with you.

- **<u>Change It Up</u>**: Regularly change your walking routine. Plan out a few different routes that you can take and mark out "safe houses" in your mind at intervals along the way. In the event of attacks, you can stop at these shops or homes where you know you will be safe. Try to incorporate these houses every time you vary your route. If you feel you are being followed, retrace your steps to the last safe location, and/or walk in the opposite direction of the person or vehicle that you are suspicious of.

- **<u>Be Paranoid and Suspicious</u>:** It is always better to be safe than sorry. When in a parking lot, look at the cars parked on either side of your vehicle. If a male in a vehicle is sitting alone in the seat nearest your car, or if you are parked next to a van, always enter your car from the side opposite the strange vehicle. If the parking lot is particularly dark or deserted, it may be wise to go back and find a friend or guard who can walk you to your car. Don't be the last person out of a location and be forced to walk alone in a dark and/or nearly empty parking lot. Look in your vehicle's back seat to insure no one is hiding there before you enter, then get in your vehicle and lock your doors immediately.

- **<u>Your best protection against rape is a good defense</u>**

If you are in a violent situation, the most important thing

is to react immediately. Continually assess the situation as it is happening. If one strategy doesn't work try a different approach. If you own a can of Mace / Pepper spray, use it. Since it is a nonlethal chemical, the spray empowers you with a weapon that doesn't require a life or death decision. Also, many such chemical defense sprays are effective from as far as ten to 15 feet away, allowing you to keep a potential attacker from getting close enough to grab you.

A WORD OF CAUTION: If you decide to carry a chemical defense spray, make sure it is a reliable, high-quality product. There are various types of chemical defense sprays available for personal protection, and some are better than others. One of the most effective is a mixture of CS tear gas and Capsicum, often used as riot control agents by the police and military. In can produce a severe burning sensation to the eyes and skin, involuntary eye closure, coughing, a choking feeling and dizziness. The effects can last up to 30 minutes, giving you time to leave the scene and call the police. Also, you should chose a spray that shoots as a stream so it is less likely to be used back against you (ie, foams can be removed from the assailant and thrown back at you causing undesired results). At Executive Defense, we have chosen to sell a spray that contains 3 components. The 3rd ingredient will mark the assailant and leave them that way for up to 48 hours without them knowing it. If the police should capture someone and look at them under florescent lighting, they will light up like a Christmas tree. You can make a purchase by visiting www.safetytrainingsystems.net or www.execdeftech.com. One more note: Don't let any self-defense weapon lull you into a false sense of security! Your best defense is to stay out of threatening situations. Common sense is the best weapon of all!

My stalker told me I have a sensitive side no one will ever know.

I have a thick skin, but I do have a vulnerable side- which found itself embroiled in a sticky situation with a text-message and telephone stalker.

He works in a coffee shop- one I used to adore but now avoid due to his creepy advances. Last night, I stood outside, debating the safety of grabbing a cup of Joe at my old hang-out. Sure enough, he was working. He almost noticed me, too. It nearly happened in slow motion. I could practically see his head turn toward mine.

Call it melodramatic, but I ducked. One red heeled shoe lifted before I had time to think. Then, almost reflexively, I bolted down the street before he saw me. Flight or fight mechanism. Close call, too. I lost a shoe, and I had to dash back to retrieve it, but he miraculously didn't see me. (But a dear friend did, and had a fantastic time laughing at me.)

The absurd lengths we must go to avoiding our unsettling admirers.

I'm not alone, either. My best friend has been harassed by a coffee-shop dweller she almost ran over in her car trying to escape. Another dear friend has had to fend off a slew of nagging older men drooling for her attention by making up a pretend friend who always requires attention, especially when it's convenient.

With the plague of frightening men infiltrating the dating scene, how's a girl to keep herself safe? It seems a single girl has to become a control freak to protect her safety. We must oversee every aspect of the interaction until we know the man well enough to be able to trust him. Wisdom and paranoia may walk hand in hand. The girl who trusts too easily is dangerously naive.

Much to my dismay, I've been struggling to regain control of the coffee shop situation for some time now.

It all began a few weeks ago when my coffee-shop admirer got my phone number. It was my fault, and it was a stupid thing to do. He was foreign, with a booming accent and a not bad sense of humor- pleasant enough initially. He wanted my phone number, which I would not give him. I told him I'd take his. I never intended to call him. But I couldn't understand his number through his accent, and in my haste to get away, he tricked me into accidentally giving mine. To get his number, I used his cell phone to call myself, which was a really, really stupid thing to do. And so began our correspondence.

He called multiple times a day. I ignored them. Then, I began receiving calls from a restricted number.

I had to answer those; I often have interviews call from blocked numbers.

I'd answer to the sound of breathing and a quick hang-up. He'd call, not blocked this time, minutes later. I ignored the calls with increasing wrath. Then, I got a text message from him telling me "the hot girl next store" will do coffee with him Friday. That made me uncomfortable. Technically, my office is very near where he works. I didn't know whether or not he was referring to me or trying (to no avail) to make me jealous. I wasn't about to find out. I quickly let him know I was glad for him and had no desire to compete. He texted me back- "In order to initiate a competition, my dear, you have to be in control of yourself." Boy, I didn't like the tone of that. I irritably assured him that I was completely in control of myself, and that this would be the end of our interaction.

He texted back a sloppy psychoanalysis about my lonely, sensitive side his texts had unearthed. I didn't respond.

Checkmate, I suppose, but running high-heeled down the street just isn't a viable long-term safety option. I'll have mace on my key chain soon, just in case.- Anonymous

56 Tips for Stalking Victims

The below represent a compilation of suggestions gathered from many victims of stalkers, law enforcement agencies, security consultants and other experts in this field. Not all will be appropriate in each and every case, and each suggestion should be considered on its own merits and on the anticipated benefit you may derive, vs. the potential negative effect each could bring about.

1. Ignore the individual
2. Be clear and unambiguous that the relationship is over, or that you do not desire a relationship
3. Do not give reasons for break up
4. Do not let the stalker see your concern
5. Cut off all contact with the stalker
6. Do not have someone else intervene in your behalf
7. Answering machine should not say "Not at Home" but rather simply state your telephone number (also use a voice other than your own on the answering machine)
8. Use caller ID or contact telephone company
9. Obtain an unlisted phone number
10. Make sure house address is clearly marked and that it is visible from the street, so police and rescue personnel can respond easily
11. Get a dog
12. Do not allow strangers in your house
13. Keep address and schedule secret
14. Inquire about laws concerning your situation

15. Notify authorities every time the stalker bothers you and keep copies of the reports
16. Treat all threats as legitimate and call police every time the stalker shows up
17. Press charges every time and have a term of his bond be that he can not contact you
18. Ask for periodic police drive-bys
19. Obtain a restraining order
20. You usually should not ask the police to go and just visit the stalker, for if the police do not arrest him, the stalker could feel that his target's best defense was useless
21. Go public
22. Send a registered letter telling person to stop; this can be sent from your attorney
23. Photograph the stalker
24. Use a video camera to tape the stalker and things that he does
25. Keep a log of stalking activities
26. Have witnesses to testify
27. Keep all written materials received from the suspect
28. Document all medical reports of physical abuse
29. Take photos of wounds, bruises and acts of vandalism
30. Join a support group
31. Vary your routine
32. Limit time spent walking alone or along the same route
33. Notify neighbors and coworkers about the situation and give them a photo of the stalker and tell them to notify you if they see him
34. If you need to, get an unlisted phone number for day to day business, and leave an answering machine on your listed or known phone number to let the unwanted person leave their messages
35. Have mail screened

36. Have coworkers screen calls and visitors (use phone mail and its mechanical-like voice answering capability)

37. Have coworkers check with each other to see if someone is calling them all

38. Alert security personnel at work

39. Stay in public areas and try not to travel alone

40. Get a cell telephone

41. Children should be accompanied to the bus or to school

42. Do not park in garages that require the keys to your car

43. Lock car door when traveling and be aware of other cars

44. Rent a mailbox from a private service

45. Ask for a free home security check-up

46. Lock fuse box, car, garage, trim hedges by windows

47. Equip gas tank with a lock and the hood release should be inside the car

48. Install deadbolts; if all the keys can not be accounted for change the locks

49. Install outside lighting (motion detectors)

50. Secure car and house at all times and install alarms in both

51. If you move, do not leave a paper trail

52. Take name off all properties and entrust them to a trusted friend or relative

53. Change jobs

54. Hire a private security guard

55. Have a contingency plan that includes:
    (a) quick access to important phone numbers
    (b) packed suitcase
    (c) reserved money Alert critical people to situation and plan

56. Take legal action other than a TRO

NOTES

5 IMPORTANT THINGS I LEARNED FROM THIS SECTION:

1. _____

2. _____

3. _____

4. _____

5. _____

IMMEDIATE ACTION STEPS THAT I WILL TAKE TODAY! :

_____

_____

_____

_____

_____

_____

_____

_____

_____

_____

_____

PART VIII

Cyber-Safety
For The Family

⚠ 1 out of 5 kids have been solicited sexually online.

⚠ 1 out of 17 kids have been harassed, threatened, or bullied.

⚠ One third of kids have been contacted by a stranger and half of these were considered inappropriate.

⚠ Most kids will not report inappropriate Internet contact to their parents because they are afraid of losing Internet privileges.

⚠ 9 out of 10 parents will never know that any inappropriate contact has occurred.

⚠ Sex, drugs and alcohol are some of the most common discussion topics.

I'm asked this question quite often from parents of my children's friends: **Should I just forbid my child from going on-line?** And if allowed online, how do I keep them safe? Do I allow my pre-teen to have a *My Space* account? How do we parent this new bit of technology?

There are dangers in every part of our society. By educating your children to these dangers and taking appropriate steps to protect them, they can benefit from the wealth of information now available on-line. With the introduction of the computer and the "world wide web" a whole new world of information, entertainment and learning opportunities have been opened up for us all. Unfortunately, "cyberspace" also holds many dangers.

To answer the question about *My Space*....I have an account and use it quite frequently for networking and business. Would I let my kids have an account? NO. What about other child friendly networking sites though? YES, we have found *Club Penguin*, *Webkinz* and *Millsbury* to be child friendly places for the kids. Two of our favorite Safety control sites are: *Cybersitter* for parental controls and *Kids Safe Mail* for our e-mail accounts (includes fun names and controls for me):

http://www.cybersitter.com/cybdefault.htm
https://www.kidsafemail.com/

So, How Do You Introduce Your Child to the Internet ?

- Explain to your child that even though he or she may be alone when using the Internet, other people can connect to your computer to find out who and where you are and that precautions must be taken.
- Explore the Internet together, letting your child take the lead.
- Talk to your child about things that concern you about the Internet ... like exploitation, pornography, hate literature and the like ... so they'll know what to do if they encounter it.

How to Control Access

- Choose an online service provider that enables you to block access to any site not marked as appropriate for children ... chat rooms, bulletin boards, news and discussion groups ... or to the Internet altogether.
- Buy software that allows you to design your own set of protective barriers to block sites and prevent your child from giving out information online.
- Look over your child's shoulder from time to time, not only checking what is on screen but also watching for uneasiness or other signs that something forbidden may be going on.

Teach Your Child to:

- Let you know right away if he or she sees anything disturbing online.
- Never give out any personal information.
- Never agree to meet someone face-to-face after encountering them online.
- Never respond to messages that contain obscene or weird language.
- Avoid sites that charge for services.
- Never send personal or family photos to anyone online without getting permission from you.

Other Ways to Promote Cyber-Safety

- Make sure Internet access at school is controlled and monitored by adults.
- If your child has a friend with Internet access, find out from that child's parents if adequate controls are in place and if children are monitored when online.
- Make sure your child's school has an Acceptable Use Policy (AUP) that defines acceptable and unacceptable online activities and resources, spells out the consequences for violations, and has a place for you and your child to sign.
- If your child receives offensive or threatening e-mail, save the material as evidence and contact your local law enforcement agency immediately.
- If you encounter a site that's inappropriate for children, send its address to online services and sites that provide blocking software so they can review it.

Internet Safety Tips For Teens (20% of children receive unwanted online solicitations)

1. Don't give out personal information about yourself, your family situation, your school, your telephone number, or your address or your activities.

2. If you become aware of the sharing, use, or viewing of child pornography online, immediately report this to the National Center for Missing & Exploited Children at 1-800-843-5678.

3. When in chat rooms remember that not everyone may be who they say they are. For example a person who says "she" is a 14-year-old girl from New York may really be a 42-year-old man from California. (Just watch *Dateline* to see the number of people like this in our country)

4. Consider volunteering at your local library, school, or Boys & Girls Club to help younger children online. Many schools and nonprofit organizations are in need of people to help set up their computers and Internet capabilities.

5. A friend you meet online may not be the best person to talk to if you are having problems at home, with your friends, or at school - remember the teenage "girl" from New York in Tip number three? Rather, find an adult in your school, church, club, or neighborhood to talk to.

6. If you are thinking about running away, a friend from online (remember the 14-year-old girl) may not be the best person to talk to or plan with. If there is no adult in your community you can find to talk to, call the National Runaway Switchboard at 1-800-621-4000. Although some of your online friends may seem to really listen to you, the Switchboard will be able to give you honest, useful answers to some of your questions about what to do when you are depressed, abused, or thinking about running away.

It is estimated that over 170 million people are connected to the Internet. Not all of them are nice people. Listed below are some links for parents who wish assistance in teaching their children about Internet Safety.

NetSmartz Workshop	A collection of age-appropriate games, videos and other materials designed for kids, teens, parents, educators and law enforcement personnel. All resources teach important lessons regarding the dangers of the Internet. Some of the teen-age material, told by teens, is pretty hard-hitting. The games may be a bit daunting for adults, but game-savvy kids should have no problems. Some resources work better with a fast Internet connection. http://www.netsmartz.org/
Internet Safety 101	About.com's introduction to Internet safety includes basic rules for keeping your kids safe online, and some suggestions on what to teach your kids about the Internet, email, and chat rooms. There are lots of explanations, for parents that aren't all that computer aware, and the suggestions are practical. The site has lots of ads, but they are worth reading around for the good information. http://familyinternet.about.com/cs/internetsafety1/a/safety01.htm
FBI - Parent's Guide to Internet Safety	Useful information, including safety suggestions, signs that your child may be at risk of exploitation on the Internet, and a glossary of Internet terms. http://www.fbi.gov/publications/pguide/pguidee.htm
CyberAngels - Parenting Your Online Child	This site includes information for parents appropriate to children of different ages, free online classes and recommendations for software that will help control and track access. Registration is required for some services. http://www.cyberangels.org/software.html

Child Safety on the Internet Highway	Guidelines from the National Center for Missing and Exploited Children. It is an older site, but the information is still good. http://www.safekids.com/child_safety.htm
NCMEC Publication Links	National Center for Missing and Exploited Children links to free publications for parents. http://www.missingkids.com

Do you know what your kids are up to online? Of course you do! You've blocked all the porn sites, set up filters, and even have a monitoring program to let you know if your kids are talking about sex, or porn, or meeting up with "uncle bob" from the chat room. You're a smart parent, but you'd be shocked if you knew what your kids were really talking about online.

There's a new trend popular among teenage chatters, and your filters won't pick up any of it. It's called l33tspeak, netspeak or just plain internet slang (leet speak from the word elite). You know what I'm talking about. Acronyms like lol, wtf, bbiab and nm. Today's kids are also lazy, and use single letter words: U replaces you, R replaces are, o replaces oh, m replaces am etc...

Less popular, but still widely used (especially in games) is true l33tspeak, which involves using numbers instead of letters. 4 replaces A, 3 replaces E, 7 replaces T 1 replaces L, and $ replaces S. These are just a few examples, some of it is worse like /V and /V\, or 13 instead of B.

Today's kids are taking their creativity to the internet, and it's affecting the way they speak. Kids (just like computer programmers) don't like to type a lot, so they try to shorten their keystrokes whenever possible. It's not only affecting the way they speak, it's starting to affect the way they write. So bad in fact, that school teachers have even reported seeing "lol" (laughing out loud) turn up on handwritten papers. (How would you pronounce that?)

Many kids as old as 17 don't know the difference between homonyms such as there, their, and they're. There aren't too many 17 year olds left who can even spell h-o-m-o-n-y-m anymore, and no it isn't spelled with an i. Remember when your high school teachers used to complain about a comma splice? Today's high school teachers are struggling to teach kids how to spell, and instant messaging isn't helping.

If you're concerned about your kids, it's absolutely crucial you learn to understand their language. Your filters may pick up porn, but do they catch the word "pron"? What about warez, which is short for illegally obtained software.

Another key phrase is the word *paw*, short for "parents are watching" or *pos* for "parents over shoulder". Every parent should be familiar with this term. Can you think of a non-naughty use for that sentence? I can't. Learn to recognize the warning signs and find out what they're doing that they don't want you to know about.

Sure you blocked porn sites, but what about Google image search? Any teenager can tell you that online image searches are the best free porn sites ever. So what can you do? Talk to your kids. Get your own copy of AOL Instant Messenger and put their names on your buddy list. Read their profiles, you'll be surprised what you find in there.

Need to find out what they're up to? Try typing their screen name, email address, name, or cell phone number into Google and see what pops up. I guarantee you'll find your son or daughter's picture, email address, and tons of should be private information about them listed on sites like hotornot.com, buddypic.com, facebattle.com, facethejury.com, or facebook.com

Does your son or daughter have a live journal or a blog? If so do you read it? You probably should. There's nothing wrong with reading their diary if they're posting it on the internet. Thousands of other people are reading it.

How much personal information are they giving to complete strangers? You'd be surprised.

As with everything else that we've discussed in this book, education along with caution and common sense are key to using the internet safely.

Top Internet Slang Phrases Every Parent Should Know:

ASL(R P) -Age Sex Location (Race / Picture)
ADR – Address
AML – All My Love
BF / GF -Boyfriend / Girlfriend
BRB -Be Right Back
CD9 - Code 9 - means parents are around
GNOC - Get Naked on Cam (webcam)
GTG - Got to Go
HAK – Hugs and Kisses
IDK - I don't know
ILU or ILY – I love you
IRL – In real life
KPC – Keep Parents clueless
(L)MIRL - (Lets) meet in real life
LOL- Laugh Out Loud
MorF - Male or Female
MOS - Mom Over Shoulder
NIFOC - Naked in Front of Computer
Noob - Newbie - often an insult to somebody who doesn't know much about something.
NMU - Not much, you?
OLL – On-line love
P911 - Parent Emergency
P&C – Private and Confidential
PAW - Parents are Watching

PIR - Parent In Room
POS - Parent Over Shoulder
PRON - Porn
PRW - Parents Are Watching
S2R - Send To Recieve (pictures)
SITD – Still in the dark
TDTM -Talk Dirty To Me
Warez - Pirated Software
W/E - Whatever
WTF - What the Fuck?
WYRN – What's your real name?

Basic Computer Safety Guidelines:

- Make your password complex – Use a combination of numbers, symbols, and letters (upper and lower case)
- Change your password regularly (every 45 to 90 days)
- Do NOT give any of your user names, passwords, or other computer / website access codes to anyone
- Do NOT open emails or attachments from strangers
- Make electronic and physical back-ups or copies of all your most important work
- Update your anti-virus software daily
- Regularly download vendor security "patches" for all of your software
- Change the manufacturer's default passwords on all of your software
- Monitor, log, and analyze successful and attempted intrusions to your systems and networks

10 Tips for Online Dating Safety

Start Slowly. Watch out for someone who seems too good to be true. Experience suggests they probably are. Begin by first communicating solely via email. Be on the lookout for odd behavior or inconsistencies. "Listen" to your correspondent's words. The person at the other end may not be who or what he/she says. Trust your instincts. If anything makes you uncomfortable, walk away for your own safety and protection.

Guard Your Anonymity. Never include your last name, real email address, personal Web site URL, home address, phone number, place of work, or any other identifying information in your profile or in the initial emails you exchange with others. Make sure your email signature file is turned off, or does not include identifying information, when corresponding with dating service member via your own email. Stop communicating with anyone who pressures you for this information or attempts in any way to trick you into revealing it. Take all the time you need to become comfortable with someone before revealing any person contact information. Ask questions and make sure you are satisfied with the answers. Trust your instincts, move cautiously and be selective. Don't feel responsible to provide personal information just because the other person does; he/she may not be honest in what they provide.

Exercise Caution and Common Sense. Careful, well-thought-out decisions generally lead to better results in dating, and this is certainly true with online dating. Guard against trusting the untrustworthy. Any potential suitor must earn your trust gradually, through consistently honorable, forthright behavior. Your job is to take all the time you need to test for a trustworthy person, and pay careful attention along the way. Take a relatively conservative approach to trusting anyone you meet online. If you think someone is lying, it is likely that they are, so act accordingly. Move on to someone you can eventually trust. Conduct yourself and your romances in a responsible manner. Don't fall in love at the click of a mouse. Don't become prematurely intimate with someone, even if that intimacy only occurs online.

Talk Via Telephone. A phone call can reveal much about a person's communication and social skills. It is worth the cost of the call to protect your security. But do not give out your personal phone number to a stranger. Try a cell phone number instead for added security. Or make arrangements to call from a pay phone so the other person's caller ID won't record your number. Only when you feel completely comfortable should you furnish your phone number.

Meet When YOU Are Ready. The beauty of meeting and relating online is that you can gradually collect information and then make a choice about pursuing the relationship in the real world. You are never obligated to meet anyone, regardless of your level of online intimacy. And even if you do decide to arrange a meeting, you always have the right to change your mind. It's possible that your decision to keep the relationship at the anonymous level is based on a hunch that you can't logically explain. Trust yourself. Go with your gut instincts, even when they can't be logically explained! Never meet someone who argues against your instincts, finds logical flaws with your feelings, or pressures you in any way.

Watch for Red Flags. Pay attention to any displays of anger, intense frustration or attempts at pressuring or controlling you. Acting in a passive-aggressive manner, making demeaning or disrespectful comments or any physically inappropriate behavior are all red flags. You should also be concerned if your date exhibits any of the following conduct without providing an acceptable explanation:

- Provides inconsistent information about age, interests, appearance, marital status, profession, employment, etc.
- Refuses to speak to you on the phone after establishing ongoing, online intimacy.
- Fails to provide direct answers to direct questions.
- Appears in person to be significantly different from his or her online persona.
- Never introduces you to friends, professional associates or family members.

Select the Safest Possible Environment. When you make the choice to meet offline, always tell someone where you are going and when you will return. Leave your date's name and telephone number with that person. Never arrange for your date to pick you up at home or where you work. Provide your own transportation, meet in a public place at a time when many people are present, and when the date is over, leave on your own as well. A familiar restaurant or coffee shop, at a time when a lot of other people will be present is often a fine choice. Avoid hikes, bike rides or drives in remote areas for the first few dates. If you decide to move to another location, take your own car. When the timing is appropriate, thank your date for getting together and say goodbye.

Take Extra Caution Outside Your Area. If you are flying in from another area, arrange for your own car and a hotel room. Do not disclose the name of your hotel and never allow your date to make the arrangements for you. Rent a car at the airport and drive directly to your hotel. Call your date from the hotel or meet at the location you have already agreed to. If the location seems inappropriate or unsafe, go back to your hotel. Try to contact your date at that location, or leave a message on voice mail or an answering machine. Always make sure a friend or family member knows your plans and has your contact information. And if possible, carry a cell phone at all times.

Get Yourself Out of a Jam. Never do anything you feel unsure about. If you are in any way afraid of your date or arrangements your date suggests, use your best judgment to diffuse the situation and get out of there. Excuse yourself long enough to call a friend for advice, ask someone else on the scene for help, or slip out the back door and drive away. If you feel you are in danger, call the police. It's always better to be safe than sorry. Never worry or feel embarrassed about your apprehensions or your behavior. Your safety is much more important than any one person's opinion of you.

While liars, cheaters and imposters certainly ply their craft on the Web, you'll also find them in nightclubs, among the membership ranks of off-line dating services, at cocktail parties, and occasionally sitting across from you at your local café. Regardless of where, or how, you meet someone, dating is never a risk-free activity. Bottom Line - A little caution will reduce your risk in these matters of the heart.

IDENTITY THEFT

It sounds like some dastardly Orwellian plot that involves making a plaster imprint of your face and fashioning silicone fingerprints and fake passports. But identity theft is an all-too-real modern-day phenomenon. According to the Federal Trade Commission, more than a half-million Americans will have their identities stolen this year.

The most common types of identity theft are:

- using or opening a credit card account fraudulently
- opening cell phone or utility accounts fraudulently
- passing bad checks or opening a new bank account
- getting loans in another person's name
- working in another person's name

Though that last one doesn't sound so bad to me (especially if they're contributing to Social Security and making their way through the items in our "to do" box), the fallout from ID theft are annoying, at best, and extremely costly and really, *really* annoying, at worst.

- One in 33 households discovered at least one type of ID theft during the previous 12 months.
- Households headed by persons age 18-24 and those with the highest incomes were the most likely victims.
- One in five victimized households spent about one month resolving problems resulting from ID theft.

(Source: "First Estimates from the National Crime Victimization Survey, Identity Theft, 2004 Bureau of Justice Statistics Bulletin)

- U.S. adult victims of identity fraud in 2005 = 9.3 million.
- In 2005, total one-year fraud amount = $54.4 billion.

(Source: Javelin Strategy and Research 2006 Identity Fraud Survey Report) www.javelinstrategy.com

The average victim will spend nearly $2,000 and 175 hours cleaning up their credit reports.

How does it happen? :

STEP 1—Getting the Identity
- The thief or thieves look for information in any number of ways
  - Discarded documents in the trash
  - Receipts from purchases
  - Lost or stolen wallets or purses
  - Online "phishing" for personal data
  - Stolen mail from mailboxes
  - Thieves are thinking of new, inventive ways every day.
- Some thieves go "wholesale" by getting lists of information on individuals through computer hacking, theft, or bribery.
- The information may be resold to other crooks or used numerous times by the original thief or thieves.
- Profits may be used to support additional criminal activities such as drug use and terrorism.

STEP 2—Exploiting the Identity
- With the information that becomes available, the thief may have false IDs made
  - A state driver's license with the thief's picture and the victim's name

- Non-driver's state license
- Social Security card
- Employer ID
- Credit cards

■ The thief may simply begin leveraging one piece of information to obtain or establish other information or assets. These may include
- New credit card accounts
- State or local licenses
- Accounts with utility companies, apartment leases, or even home mortgages.

STEP 3—Discovering the Theft
■ The thief continues to build a "persona" using the victim's name, good credit, and even good character references. The thief never pays the bills, but the victim is left with a bad name and ruined credit.
■ Eventually, the victim tries to get a new credit account and is turned down, or gets a bill for a credit card he or she never owned, or starts getting calls from bill collectors.
■ The thief might abandon the victim's identity because he or she has "spoiled" the name of the victim (e.g., with a criminal offense or bankruptcy).
■ When the crime or ruined credit is discovered, the victim is left to clean up the mess.

Who is vulnerable?

People who
■ Keep their money in bank accounts
■ Use credit or debit cards
■ Generate trash with unshredded paper in it
■ Casually toss credit card or other receipts into public receptacles

- Get personal bills by mail or electronically
- Don't check their credit card reports and bank statements
- Don't regularly check their credit bureau reports
- Have accessible mail boxes

Although identity theft is impossible to completely prevent, the following tips can help mitigate this threat:

14 Identity Protection Tips

1. Guard your social security number. It is the key to your credit report and bank accounts, and is the prime target of criminals.
2. Monitor your credit report. It contains your Social Security number (SSN), present and prior employers, a listing of all account numbers, including those that have been closed, and your overall credit score.
3. Shred all old bank and credit statements, as well as "junk mail" credit-card offers, before trashing them.
4. Remove your name from the marketing lists of the three credit-reporting bureaus. This reduces the number of pre-approved credit offers you receive.
5. Add your name to the National Do Not Call registry list: www.donotcall.gov.
6. Do not carry extra credit cards or other important identity documents except when needed.
7. Photocopy both sides of your license & credit cards so you have all the account numbers, expiration dates and phone numbers if you lose these items.
8. Consider not mailing bill payments and checks from home. They can be stolen from your mailbox and your checks washed clean in chemicals. Instead take them to a postal drop box.
9. Have your SSN removed from your personal

checks, drivers licenses & medical ID cards.

10. Order your Social Security Earnings and Benefits statement once a year to check for fraud. Official Web Site: (www.socialsecurity.gov/statement).

11. Examine the charges on your credit-card statements before paying them.

12. Cancel unused credit-card accounts. Obtain your credit report to identify current accounts.

13. Never give your credit-card number or personal information over the phone unless you have initiated the call and trust that business.

Consider subscribing to a credit-report monitoring service that will notify you whenever.

Finally, it is sad to note that of the 10 million people a year who are affected by identity theft, not all of these thieves are "strangers". Yes, most identity theft does happen at work and can happen in seconds because we tend to be trusting of those around us but what would you do if you were victimized by a family member? My best friend's father (a SR.) was using his name and SS# since the time he was very small, completely ruining his credit. A recent report on the news reported another such story and his final outcome of being one of only a handful of people to finally be issued a new SS#. Dr Phil just aired a show on brothers who have stolen their sibling's ID and used it for selfish purposes. Bottom line: Keep your information safe guarded, run a check of your credit every so often and run one on your children – they SHOULD NOT have anything to report and if they do, fix it NOW someone is impersonating them and it could ruin their future as a consumer!

Online Resources

- Federal Trade Commission: www.ftc.gov
- Department of Justice:
  www.usdoj.gov/criminal/fraud/idtheft.html
- Better Business Bureau: www.bbb.org
- United States Postal Service: www.usps.com
- National Criminal Justice Reference Service:
  www.ncjrs.gov

Credit reporting services: Report the theft with each of the three major credit bureaus (they all have fraud centers). Ask that a "fraud alert" be placed on your file. Also request that no new lines of credit be granted without first seeking your approval. You'll be asked to record the incident(s) in writing, and include copies of any documents (e.g., a police report, correspondence with your bank or other creditors) to be used as evidence. Here's contact information for each major credit bureau:

Equifax (http://www.equifax.com/), P.O. Box 740241, Atlanta, GA 30374-0241; report fraud by calling (800) 525-6285

Experian (formerly TRW, http://www.experian.com/), P.O. Box 1017, Allen, TX 75013; report fraud by calling (800) 301-7195

TransUnion (http://www.transunion.com/), Fraud Victim Assistance Division, P.O. Box 6790, Fullerton, CA 92634; report fraud by calling (800) 680-7289

Your Credit

Credit monitoring is a service in which an authorized agency notifies you whenever an update is made to your credit report, such as the opening or closing of an account, a change in address, or the processing of a loan payment. It's a great way to keep track of your credit standing. It's also one of the only ways to catch identity theft early, before any serious damage is done. Identity theft is the fastest-growing crime nationwide, affecting an estimated 10 million Americans last year alone.

How can I improve my credit score?

- Reduce your debt-to-credit ratio. Avoid leaving your account balances near the maximum credit limit, even if you can do so and still remain well within your budget. Credit bureaus interpret this as a sign that you are borrowing almost as much as you can handle, which they assume makes you a higher risk. A good rule of thumb is to keep your balances below 50% of your credit limit.
- Correct errors in your report. These are surprisingly common. A utility company or lender could mistakenly report one of your payments as late, which could adversely affect your credit rating until you correct it. Be advised that correcting an error can take as long as 90 days, so it helps to monitor your credit report and fix mistakes early.
- Make all your payments on time. This is particularly important in the months before you plan to apply for a loan or job when an employer might check your credit report. Why? A recent late payment will affect your score more than, say, a late payment from several years ago.
- Consider leaving old accounts open, even if you don't use them much anymore. The length of your credit history - how long you've been borrowing - is a factor in your credit score, so it pays to keep these accounts alive. Also, closing an account will reduce the total amount you can borrow, which increases your debt-to-credit ratio.
- Pay off debt rather than shuffling it between

accounts. Unless you are severely behind in debt and are taking steps to resolve it, closing some of your accounts will adversely affect your debt-to-credit ratio.

NOTES

5 IMPORTANT THINGS I LEARNED FROM THIS SECTION:

1. _____

2. _____

3. _____

4. _____

5. _____

IMMEDIATE ACTION STEPS THAT I WILL TAKE TODAY! :

_____

_____

_____

_____

_____

_____

_____

_____

_____

_____

PART IX

Protecting Your Business

PROTECTING YOUR BUSINESS

<u>Burglary</u>

In the U.S. alone, a commercial robbery is committed every four minutes. That's more than 100,000 robberies each year.
65% of nonresidential burglaries occur during the nighttime.

- Light all exterior points of entry with permanent fixtures that are difficult to reach or tamper with.
- Light the interior of your business enough that someone outside the building could see someone inside.
- Install a fence or hedge – it's your first line of defense.
  - You should be able to see through the fence.
  - Hedges should be wide, rather than high, and of a prickly, thorny variety.
- Install window locks designed and positioned so they cannot be reached and unlocked after breaking the glass.
- Install safety glass (glazing). It is highly effective at deterring break-ins.
- Install motion detectors to sense movement inside the building.
- Install entry protecting alarms to detect the breaking of windows and the opening of doors.
- Install point protectors (such as pressure-switch

mats) to detect when someone enters a restricted area, such as by a cash register.
- Install a deadbolt lock/latch in each exterior door.
- Lock overhead and receiving doors with high-quality padlocks.

Internal Theft

Your employees are 15 times more likely to steal from you than your customers.
- Screen all employees before hiring them – it's the best defense against internal theft.
- Never have fewer than two people close up at night.
- Have all keys distributed to employees engraved with the words "Do Not Duplicate."
- Watch for warning signs – employees who:
    o Are living beyond their means
    o Habitually violate company policies
    o Have a substance abuse problem
    o Are chronic liars
    o Seem immature or troubled
    o May have cause to feel wronged
- Never rule anyone out – anyone could be a thief.
- Use a card access system rather than traditional keys – access cards can't easily be duplicated.
- Install a closed-circuit television system. It allows you to monitor employees and serves as a very strong deterrent when employees know one is in place.

Retail
Supervise the Selling Floor

1. Be on the sales floor at least 80 percent of the day.
2. When walking the floor, continually observe and respond to mismarked merchandise, incorrect price

signs, unattended price gun, loose price tickets, open showcases, unlocked security fixtures, empty packages, known shoplifters, suspicious customers, merchandise concealed for later pickup, merchandise without security tags, inoperative security equipment, salespeople not following procedures, fitting room attendants off their post, customers not being serviced, cashiers not properly ringing sales, coupons not controlled, loose bags or gift boxes accessible to customers, security tape not secured, guards not attentive to their duties, unpaid-for merchandise under wrap desks, employee handbags under counters, unauthorized checks or voids or refunds . . . and more.

3. Encourage employees to keep their heads up and eyes open.
4. Help employees to do a good job and take pride in their accomplishments.

Give Shoplifters an Uneasy Feeling

1. Instruct employees to greet or acknowledge every customer who enters their department.
2. Provide personal customer service to as many customers as possible.
3. Instruct floor personnel to make frequent eye contact with customers who wish to browse on their own.
4. Assign zones for staff coverage so that floor personnel don't leave vulnerable areas unattended.
5. Instruct floor personnel to make a pleasant comment to every customer about the item(s) being taken into the fitting room, so that the customer is aware of what is expected to be either returned or purchased.
6. Maintain 100 percent compliance when placing

security tags on vulnerable merchandise.

7. Install added security measures in "blind spots" around the store (e.g., bright lighting, security mirrors, anti-shoplifting signs, and camera).

8. Lower displays around the cash register that block the cashier's view of the selling floor.

9. If your store is large in size, make frequent announcements over the public address (PA) system, such as "Security to area 4," even if your store doesn't have security personnel or an area 4.

10. Issue a criminal trespass warning to all known shoplifters who you want to be prohibited (by law) from entering your store again. Let shoplifters know, by work and deed, that your store prosecutes all offenders.

11. Encourage a close working relationship between employees and loss prevention personnel.

Reduce Opportunities for Employee Theft

1. Only authorize a refund in the presence of the customer.

2. Go behind the counter to authorize a void or "over ring" so you can observe potential problems (e.g., bagged merchandise which could be handed out to friends, consumables not paid for, money not in its proper slot in the till or too much cash in the drawer).

3. Sign voids or "over rings" only while the customer is present.

4. Inspect trash dumpster at random but at least weekly, following trash collection but prior to pickup.

5. Don't allow employees to write up, ring up or wrap purchases for themselves or relatives.

6. Review cash over/short reports every day and

respond appropriately.

7. Provide employees with lockers or other secure area for employee handbags, purchases, coats and other belongings that are prohibited on the sales floor.

8. Require at least two employees to open and close the store, simultaneously.

9. Never allow merchandise to leave the store "on approval," without being purchased first.

10. Prohibit hand-carried merchandise transfers from being taken out of the store without proper paperwork.

11. Instruct all employees to enter and leave through a designated employee door.

12. Require managers and employees to always present their belongings for inspection before leaving.

13. Require that all merchandise to be taken out of the store for alteration, cleaning, style show or other purpose, be signed in and out and authorized on a merchandise control log.

14. Do not allow employees to wear store merchandise not purchased.

15. Prohibit employees from browsing behind counters or in back areas of departments that they don't work or sell in.

16. Prohibit employees from trying on merchandise without the knowledge of a manager or other supervisor.

17. Never allow only one person to write the sale, ring it up, wrap the merchandise and ship it out of the store.

18. Secure all shipping labels unless part of an authorized, register-validated sales receipt.

19. Don't allow wrapped merchandise to be hand delivered to UPS or the post office unless authorized and recorded on a store delivery log.

20. Limit employee access to markdown pens and

remarking machines when access is not needed.

21. Limit the number of employees authorized to ring up other employees' sales, reducing the opportunities for collusion.
22. Require management authorization of employee purchase transactions.
23. Occasionally offer to assist employees in completing a customer transaction to verify that the amount paid and the merchandise in the bag is correct (particularly when suspicious).
24. Never allow employees to work with an open cash drawer. They must close the register drawer before ringing the next sale.
25. Limit the number of "NO SALE" rings by defining under what special conditions they will be permitted.
26. Review daily exception reports highlighting excessive voids, over rings, no sales, refunds and other suspicious activity.
27. Require all receipts to be given to customers.
28. Require employees to immediately destroy (i.e., tear twice in half) any receipts left by a customer.
29. Prohibit employees from using another employee's I.D. number for any purpose whatsoever.
30. Prohibit cashiers from taking a reading on their cash register. If register readings cannot be done by a supervisor, require cashiers to count their cash, enter the amount on the register and place the cash in a locked deposit bag before taking a reading.
31. Don't allow register transaction numbers to be cleared by anyone at the end of the day. They should continue ad infinitum to ensure that the register tape was not removed from the register.
32. Prohibit the possession of keys to bank deposit bags when the bank is responsible for opening locked deposit bags. There should be no reason for

managers or anyone to open a locked deposit bag, whether full or empty.

33. Make bank deposit drops daily . . . no exceptions.
34. Limit access to keys which disarm the fire exit(s) security crash bar alarm(s).
35. Keep perimeter doors alarmed during night-fill operation and when the store is not open to customers. Supervisor authorization should be required to leave the store.
36. Change door cores on locks to the store when key holders are transferred, leave voluntarily or are terminated.
37. Require bottle return refunds over $3.00 to be co-signed at the time of the transaction by someone who is required to "eyeball" the number of bottles returned as compared with the amount of the refund slip.
38. Require employees to keep the receipt for merchandise they consume in the store during that day, for possible verification by the manager.
39. Tell employees what will happen if anyone is caught stealing . . . not what can happen, but what will happen.

Promote a Theft-Free Culture

1. Include questions on personal integrity in the pre-employment screening process to let prospective employees know that integrity is an important issue to your company.
2. Start employees on the right foot by welcoming them to the company, giving them written rules of conduct and describing the risks and consequences involved in dishonesty so that they may make the right decision for themselves, should they ever find themselves in a compromising position.
3. Don't treat employees like criminals, so they feel

mistrusted and unappreciated.

4. Give employees a reason to value their job based on what they do and how they are treated.
5. Encourage Loss Prevention to watch employees less and work with employees more.
6. Remind employees that it is better to try and prevent a theft than try and catch people.
7. Train employees how to say "NO" when friends or relatives ask for extra merchandise, a lower price or an employee discount. Each employee should be instructed in advance about what to say when put in such a compromising situation.
8. Explain to employees why employee theft in a store causes a problem for co-workers (e.g., managers begin to distrust everyone, innocent co-workers may be implicated, tighter internal controls are installed, the manager may lose his job, all employees may be replaced).
9. Make it easier for employees to come forward to report their suspicions or concerns:
   1. Tell employees what to report and when to report it
   2. Tell employees exactly how the information they provide will be used
   3. Give employees alternative ways to report their suspicions (i.e., by telephone, in writing or in person)
   4. Reassure employees that they are doing the right thing

Encourage Employee Involvement

1. Remember that the attitude and performance of store employees is heavily influenced by the attitude and performance of store management.
2. Treat employees with respect and consideration.

3. Although the customer is king, never treat customers better than employees.
4. Keep employees well informed about what's happening in their department and the store, so they feel more a part of the company.
5. Make yourself accessible to employees.
6. Be friendly and show your appreciation. Say "good morning" and "thank you" to people.
7. Reduce unnecessary stress on the job. Employees should not be continually subjected to excessive workload pressure, unreasonable demands, constant criticism or frequent threats by managers or supervisors.
8. Make it easy for employees to call the manager of security for assistance by silent alarm, intercom or telephone.
9. Drop everything and respond immediately when you receive an employee call for assistance.
10. Don't criticize employees who may be over-cautious.
11. Train employees what to look for and how to respond to a potential shoplifting situation, in a manner which will not cause employees to fear becoming involved in a confrontation or lawsuit.
12. Remind employees to observe the physical symptoms and behavioral changes associated with drug use.
13. Train employees that internal theft can never be a big problem when the other employees (by speaking up) don't allow it to happen.
14. Catch employees at doing things right, rather than only looking for what they do wrong.
15. Remember that getting employees involved in loss prevention can be an easy thing to do because it will always become one of their priorities when it becomes one of yours.

Other Threats:

Liability - More and more, businesses need to protect against lawsuits and false insurance claims brought by customers as well as employees.

Vendor Theft Delivery shortages are very common. Have your employees count every item delivered.

Employee Productivity Otherwise honest employees stole $160 billion last year by wasting time on the job.

Poor Customer Service The average customer service incident results in the loss of a minimum of 10 customers.

Fraud Customers are less likely to commit credit card and merchandise return fraud when there is an obvious video surveillance system in place.

Sample OSHA Report
Violence Incident Report Forms:

Sample:

The following items serve merely as an example of what might be used or modified by employers to help prevent workplace violence (Sample/Draft – Adapt to your own location and business circumstances)

Confidential Incident Report
To:
Date of Incident:
Day of week:
Time:
Assailant: ___Female ___Male
Location of Incident: (Map/sketch on reverse side or attached):
From:
Phone:

Nature of the Incident: ("x" to all applicable boxes)
- o Preventative or Warning Report
- o Bomb or terrorist type threat
- o Transportation accident
- o Contacts with objects or equipment
- o Falls
- o Exposures
- o Fire or explosion
- o Other

Violence Directed Toward:
- o Co-worker
- o Supervisor
- o Visitor

Assailant:
- o Staff
- o Supervisor
- o Visitor

Assailant's Name:

Assailant:
- o Armed
- o Un-armed

Predisposing Factors:
- o Intoxication
- o Dissatisfied with care / waiting time
- o Grief reaction
- o Prior history of violence
- o Gang related
- o Other (describe)

Description of Incident:
- o Physical Abuse
- o Verbal Abuse
- o Other

Injuries:
- o Yes
- o No

Extent of Injuries:

Detailed Description of the Incident:

Did Any Person Leave the Area Because of the Incident?

Present at Time of Incident?

Police Involved?

Other Security Involved?

Termination of Incident:
- o Incident diffused
- o Police Notified
- o Assailant Arrested

Disposition of Assailant:
- o Stayed on Premises
- o Escorted off Premises
- o Left on Own
- o Other

Restraints Used:
- o Yes
- o No
- o Type:

Report completed by and Title:
Witnesses:

Source: Reprinted with permission of Karen Smith Keinbaum, Esq., Counsel to the Law Firm of Abbott, Nicholson, Quilter, Esshaki & Youngblood, P.C., **Detroit, MI**

NOTES

5 IMPORTANT THINGS I LEARNED FROM THIS SECTION:

1. _____

2. _____

3. _____

4. _____

5. _____

IMMEDIATE ACTION STEPS THAT I WILL TAKE TODAY! :

_____

_____

_____

_____

_____

_____

_____

_____

_____

_____

PART X

The People Side Of Emergency Preparedness

Tornadoes

The following are facts about tornadoes:

- They may strike quickly, with little or no warning.
- They may appear nearly transparent until dust and debris are picked up or a cloud forms in the funnel.
- The average tornado moves Southwest to Northeast, but tornadoes have been known to move in any direction.
- The average forward speed of a tornado is 30 MPH, but may vary from stationary to 70 MPH.
- Tornadoes can accompany tropical storms and hurricanes as they move onto land.
- Waterspouts are tornadoes that form over water.
- Tornadoes are most frequently reported east of the Rocky Mountains during spring and summer months.
- Peak tornado season in the southern states is March through May; in the northern states, it is late spring through early summer.
- Tornadoes are most likely to occur between 3 p.m. and 9 p.m., but can occur at any time Be alert to changing weather conditions:
- Listen to NOAA Weather Radio or to commercial radio or television newscasts for the latest information.

- Look for approaching storms.
- Look for the following danger signs:
  - Dark, often greenish sky
  - Large hail
  - A large, dark, low-lying cloud (particularly if rotating)
  - Loud roar, similar to a freight train.
  -

If you see approaching storms or any of the danger signs, be prepared to take shelter
immediately. If you are under a tornado WARNING, seek shelter immediately!

If you are in:

- A structure (e.g. residence, small building, school, nursing home, hospital, factory, shopping center, high-rise building)

THEN:

- Go to a pre-designated shelter area such as a safe room, basement, storm cellar, or the lowest building level. If there is no basement, go to the center of an interior room on the lowest level (closet, interior hallway) away from corners, windows, doors, and outside walls. Put as many walls as possible between you and the outside. Get under a sturdy table and use your arms to protect your head and neck. Do not open windows.

If you are in:

- A vehicle, trailer, or mobile home

THEN:

- Get out immediately and go to the lowest floor of a sturdy, nearby building or a storm shelter. Mobile homes, even if tied down, offer little protection from tornadoes.

If you are outside with no shelter THEN:

- Lie flat in a nearby ditch or depression and cover your head with your hands. Be aware of the potential for flooding.
- Do not get under an overpass or bridge. You are safer in a low, flat location. Never try to outrun a tornado in urban or congested areas in a car or truck. Instead, leave the vehicle immediately for safe shelter.
- Watch out for flying debris. Flying debris from tornadoes causes most fatalities and injuries.

Hurricanes

June through November marks hurricane season. Basically, the whole shoreline of the East Coast is threatened when a hurricane blows in.

To prepare for a hurricane, you should take the following measures:

- Make plans to secure your property. Permanent storm shutters offer the best protection for windows. A second option is to board up windows with 5/8" marine plywood, cut to fit and ready to install. Tape does not prevent windows from breaking.
- Install straps or additional clips to securely fasten your roof to the frame structure. This will reduce roof damage.
- Be sure trees and shrubs around your home are well trimmed.
- Clear loose and clogged rain gutters and downspouts.

Here are some guidelines to help you stay safe if a hurricane threatens.

- By late May, recheck your supply of boards, tools, batteries, non- perishable foods and other items you may need during a hurricane.

- Listen to the latest weather reports and official notices. This will give you advance notice, sometimes before watches and warnings are issued. Keep a battery-powered radio on hand in case the power goes out.

- If your area comes under a hurricane watch, continue normal activities but stay tuned to the Weather Channel or to a local radio station and ignore rumors.

- If your area receives a hurricane warning, stay calm. Leave low- lying areas that may be swept by high tides or storm waves. If there's time, secure mobile homes before leaving for more substantial shelter. Move automobiles to high ground as both sound and sea can flood even central spots on the Outer Banks.

- Moor boats securely or haul them out of the water to a safe place.

- Board up windows or protect them with storm shutters. (Though some people recommend using tape on windows, many experts and most locals will tell you tape isn't strong enough to work and it's very difficult to remove). Secure outdoor objects that might blow away such as garbage cans, outdoor furniture, tools, etc. that may become dangerous missiles in high winds. If the items can't be tied down, bring them inside.

- Store drinking water in clean bathtubs, jugs or bottles since water supplies can become contaminated by hurricane floods.

- Be sure you have lots of flashlights, batteries, a battery-operated radio, and perhaps emergency cooking facilities.

- Keep your car fueled since service stations may be inoperable for several days following a storm.
- Stay indoors during a storm, and keep your pets inside too. Do not attempt to travel by foot or car. Monitor weather conditions and don't be fooled by the calm of the hurricane's eye. The storm isn't over yet!
- Stay out of disaster areas unless you are qualified to help. Your presence might hamper rescue work.
- If necessary, seek medical attention at the nearest Red Cross disaster station or health center.
- Do not travel except in an emergency such as transporting someone who is injured. Be careful along debris-filled streets and highways. Roads may be under- mined and could collapse under the weight of the car. Floodwater could hide dangerous holes in the road.
- Avoid loose and dangling wires. Report them to North Carolina Power or the police.
- Report broken sewer or water mains to the county or town water department.
- Be careful not to start fires. Lowered water pressure may make fire fighting difficult.
- Stay away from rivers and streams.
- Check roofs, windows and outdoor storage areas for wind or water damage.
- Do not let young children or your pets outside immediately after a storm. There are numerous dangers like fallen power lines and wild animals that have been disoriented because of the storm.

Remember, you already possess the most important safety tool - common sense. Use it often and you're sure to stay safe!

Don't forget that "common sense" when it comes to the use of portable generators either. Portable generators are useful when temporary or remote electric power is needed, but they also can be hazardous. The primary hazards to avoid when using a generator are carbon monoxide (CO) poisoning from the toxic engine exhaust, electric shock or electrocution, fire and burns. Every year, people die in incidents related to portable generator use. Most of the incidents associated with portable generators reported to CPSC involve CO poisoning from generators used indoors or in partially-enclosed spaces. When used in a confined space, generators can produce high levels of CO within minutes. When you use a portable generator, remember that you cannot see or smell CO. Even if you do not smell exhaust fumes, you may still be exposed to CO. If you start to feel sick, dizzy, or weak while using a generator, get to fresh air RIGHT AWAY. DO NOT DELAY. The CO from generators can rapidly kill you.

Create a Family Disaster Plan

Meet with your family:

- Discuss the types of disasters that could occur in your community (hurricane, flood, tornado, hazardous materials spill)
- Explain how to prepare and respond
- Discuss what to do if advised to evacuate
- Practice what you have discussed
- Plan how your family will stay in contact if separated by disaster
- Pick two meeting places
    1. A location a safe distance from your home

in case of fire
2. A place outside your neighborhood in case you can't return home

- Choose an "out-of-state" friend as a "check-in-contact" for everyone to call
- Post emergency numbers by every telephone
- Show responsible family members how and when to shut off water, gas and electricity at main switches
- Install a smoke detector on each level of your home, especially near bedrooms; test monthly and change batteries two times each year
- Make a small fire extinguisher available on each floor of your house and a ladder for escape from the second story of your home
- Contact your local American Red Cross Chapter and learn first aid and CPR
- Meet with your neighbors and plan how your neighborhood can work together after a disaster. Know your neighbor's skills (medical, technical). Consider how you could help neighbors with special needs, such as elderly or disabled persons. Make plans for child care in case parents can't get home.
- **<u>Remember to practice and maintain your plan.</u>**

Pet Guidelines

Animals also are affected by disasters. Use the guidelines below to prepare a plan for caring for pets and large animals.
Plan for pet disaster needs by:

- Identifying shelter.
- Gathering pet supplies.
- Ensuring your pet has proper ID and up-to-date

veterinarian records.
- Providing a pet carrier and leash.

Take the following steps to prepare to shelter your pet:

- Call your local emergency management office, animal shelter, or animal control office to get advice and information.
- Keep veterinary records to prove vaccinations are current.
- Find out which local hotels and motels allow pets and where pet boarding facilities are located. Be sure to research some outside your local area in case local facilities close.

Know that, with the exception of service animals, pets are not typically permitted in emergency shelters as they may affect the health and safety of other occupants.

Items To Have In Your Basic Survival Kit

As we witnessed the devastation caused by Katrina, many of us have wondered what we would do if we were faced with the same situation. Families should prepare for the worst and pray for the best. In addition to a disaster survival kit, having an Emergency Grab-and-Go File is one of the most important things you can do to ensure that in times of stress, emergency or grief, you are not compounding the situation by not knowing where important documents and contact information are. *The following items are recommended for inclusion in your basic disaster kit as well as your Emergency Grab-and-Go Kit:*

Store at least a three-day supply of non-perishable food. Select foods that require no refrigeration, preparation or cooking, and little or no water. Select food items that are compact and lightweight.

<u>Foods in your Disaster Survival Kit:</u>

- Ready-to-eat canned meats, fruits, and vegetables
- Canned juices
- Staples (salt, sugar, pepper, spices, etc.)
- High energy foods
- Vitamins
- Food for infants
- • Comfort/stress foods

<u>First Aid Kit</u>
<u>Assemble a first aid kit for your home and one for each</u>
<u>car.</u>

- (20) adhesive bandages, various sizes.
- 5" x 9" sterile dressing.
- conforming roller gauze bandage.
- triangular bandages.
- 3 x 3 sterile gauze pads.
- 4 x 4 sterile gauze pads.
- roll 3" cohesive bandage.
- germicidal hand wipes or waterless alcohol-based hand sanitizer.
- (6) antiseptic wipes.
- pair large medical grade non-latex gloves.
- Adhesive tape, 2" width.
- Anti-bacterial ointment.
- Cold pack.
- Scissors (small, personal).
- Tweezers.
- CPR breathing barrier, such as a face shield.

- Non-Prescription Drugs.
- Aspirin or nonaspirin pain reliever.
- Anti-diarrhea medication.
- Antacid (for stomach upset).
- Syrup of Ipecac (use to induce vomiting if advised by the Poison Control Center).
- Laxative.
- Activated charcoal (use if advised by the Poison Control Center).

For Baby

- • Formula
- Diapers
- Bottles
- Powdered milk
- Medications
- **For Adults**
- Heart and high blood pressure medication
- Insulin
- Prescription drugs
- Denture needs
- Contact lenses and supplies
- Extra eye glasses
- Entertainment (games and books)

<u>Tools and Supplies:</u>

- Mess kits, or paper cups, plates, and plastic utensils
- Emergency preparedness manual
- Battery-operated radio and extra batteries
- Flashlight and extra batteries
- Cash or traveler's checks, change
- Non-electric can opener, utility knife

- Fire extinguisher: small canister ABC type
- Tube tent
- Pliers
- Tape
- Compass
- Matches in a waterproof container
- Aluminum foil
- Plastic storage containers
- Signal flare
- Paper, pencil
- Needles, thread
- Medicine dropper
- Shut-off wrench, to turn off household gas and water
- Whistle
- Plastic sheeting
- Map of the area (for locating shelters)
- Sanitation
- Toilet paper, towelettes
- Soap, liquid detergent
- Feminine supplies
- Personal hygiene items
- Plastic garbage bags, ties (for personal sanitation uses)
- Plastic bucket with tight lid
- Disinfectant
- Household chlorine bleach
- Clothing and Bedding
- Include at least one complete change of clothing and footwear per person.
- Sturdy shoes or work boots
- Rain gear
- Blankets or sleeping bags
- Hat and gloves

- Thermal underwear
- Sunglasses
- Special Items

Remember family members with special requirements, such as infants and elderly or disabled persons

Documents
Create a Grab-and-Go File Containing (Keep these records in a waterproof, portable container):

Legal Information

- Copy of Living Will and Location of the original version
- Copy of Will and Location of original version
- Power of Attorney Health Care
- Details of Trusts / Judgments for and against you
- Estate Arrangements

Store your kit in a convenient place known to all family members. Keep a smaller version of the supplies kit in the trunk of your car.

Identification Information

- Social Security Card and Related Information
- Birth and death Certificates
- Marriage and Divorce Documents
- Education certificates / degrees, etc
- Copies of the front and back of all cards in family members' wallets

Important Names and Contact Information

- Name, address and phone number of your nearest relative or friend
- Doctors: medical doctor, dentist, eye doctor, chiropractor, etc
- Insurance agency / agent
- Accountant or bookkeeper
- Investment broker and file location
- Insurance Details

Personal Information & Photos

- Wedding and/or baby photos
- Current photos of all family members
- Important medical information such as allergies
- Prescription medication you are on
- Location of Important Documents not in the file
- Location of Valuables

Employment and Benefit Information

- Include names, numbers and contact information
- Income sources – from what location and frequency

Banking account numbers and contact information

- Banking / Credit Union Information
- Retirement Fund(s) Information
- Savings Information
- Mortgage Documents

Keep items in airtight plastic bags. Change your stored water supply every six months so it stays fresh. Replace your stored food every six months. Re-think your kit and family needs at least once a year. Replace batteries, update clothes, etc. Ask your physician or pharmacist about storing prescription medications.

If you live in a cold climate, you must think about warmth. It is possible that you

will not have heat. Think about your clothing and bedding supplies. Be sure to

include one complete change of clothing and shoes per person, including:

- Jacket or coat.
- Long pants.
- Long sleeve shirt.
- Sturdy shoes.
- Hat, mittens, and scarf.
- Sleeping bag or warm blanket (per person).

Just as important as putting your supplies together is maintaining them so they are

safe to use when needed. Here are some tips to keep your supplies ready and in

good condition:

- Keep canned foods in a dry place where the temperature is cool.
- Store boxed food in tightly closed plastic or metal containers to protect from pests and to extend its shelf life.
- Throw out any canned good that becomes swollen, dented, or corroded.
- Use foods before they go bad, and replace them with fresh supplies.
- Place new items at the back of the storage area and older ones in the front.
- Change stored food and water supplies every six

months. Be sure to write the date you store it on all containers.

- Re-think your needs every year and update your kit as your family needs change.
- Keep items in airtight plastic bags and put your entire disaster supplies kit in one or two easy-to-carry containers, such as an unused trashcan, camping backpack, or duffel bag.

NOTES

5 IMPORTANT THINGS I LEARNED FROM THIS SECTION:

1. _____

2. _____

3. _____

4. _____

5. _____

IMMEDIATE ACTION STEPS THAT I WILL TAKE TODAY! :

_____

_____

_____

_____

_____

_____

_____

_____

_____

_____

_____

PART XI

Gangs in the Street

Gang Definitions

There are thousands of gang members and wannabees living in rural and urban cities throughout our nation. However, the gang problem is only evident in cities that choose to acknowledge the problem. The feeling of denial that so many community and law enforcement administrators display towards their growing problems of drugs, gangs and school violence is amazing. Many are quick to say, "Yeah, we have gangs in our city, but they are nothing like the ones you deal with in California." *No matter where members are located, there isn't* a difference in their mentality, lack of values, goals or interest in the criminal lifestyle.

There is no difference between a 14 year old in Los Angeles and a small Wisconsin town if they both share the same interest, desire and commitment to the gang lifestyle. With so many new criminal trends continually bombarding law enforcement, such as identity theft, computer crimes, school shootings, drug labs and threats of terrorism, the growth of gangs within the Hispanic immigrant population is a spreading plague that is growing unnoticed in many rural areas and once rooted, quickly strangles a city's resources, giving them little time to react. According to the 2005 National Gang Trends Survey, Hispanic gangs are the fastest growing gang group, particularly in the immigrant population. The growth of gangs in immigrant neighborhoods is not a new phenomenon. However, the rapid growth of Hispanic gangs, especially in rural America is a relatively new trend.

Lack of parental supervision is a major problem. Another dilemma is a lack of understanding of the English language. This creates a unique dependency on the child, giving the child more authority and power over the adults. Many immigrant families understand little of the American culture. As a result, some view their child's gang affiliation as typical American teen behavior. Because all their child's friends may be a part of a gang, the parents accept the dress, talk and behavior as normal teenage behavior. So what exactly is a gang, what signs should we look for, and why should we be concerned?

A street gang is:

- three or more people,
- who share a unique name or have identifiable marks or symbols, (such as tattoos, wearing certain styles of clothing, colors, hairstyles, graffiti, etc.)
- associate together on a regular basis and sometimes claim a specific location or territory,
- have an identifiable organization or hierarchy, (although the leader for one type of criminal activity may be different from that of another criminal activity), and either individually or collectively engage in antisocial, unlawful or criminal activity in an effort to further the gang's social or economical status.

Common Crimes Committed by Gang Members:

- Murder - The intentional killing of a person.
- Manslaughter - The unintentional killing of a person.
- Forcible Rape - Compulsory sexual intercourse by use or threat of physical force.
- Robbery - Theft by use or threat of physical force.

(Physical injury to the victim is not necessary.)

- Terrorist Threats & Witness Intimidation - The threat of physical force or death and the present ability to complete the threat.
- Extortion - To obtain property from another with their consent induced by force or fear.
- Aggravated Assault - A physical attack intended to inflict serious bodily harm. (Physical injury to the victim is not necessary.)
- Simple Assault - A physical attack intended to inflict any bodily harm. (Physical injury to the victim is not necessary.)
- Burglary - The unlawful entry of a building in order to commit a crime.
- Larceny or Theft - The unlawful taking of property without use or threat of physical harm.
- Grand Theft Auto - The unlawful taking of a vehicle without use or threat of physical harm.
- Carjacking - The unlawful taking of a vehicle with the use or threat of physical force. (Physical injury to the victim is not necessary.)
- Drug Trafficking or Sales - Possession of a controlled substance with intent to distribute..
- Drug Possession - Possession of a controlled substance without intent to sell.
- Vandalism - The intentional destruction of another's property.
- Arson - The intentional destruction of another's property by fire or burning.
- Public Disorder - A variety of offenses such as disorderly conduct, public intoxication or loitering.

Gangs:

Gang members communicate in many different ways. Speech is the most obvious; however, gang members also make use of nonverbal methods of exchanging thoughts. Gang members have their own language, which contains phrases, hand signs, tattoos, markings and graffiti. These often overlap. As a parent, you may not recognize them right away.

- Bloods: Originally from Los Angeles, the Bloods are one of the largest associations of street gangs in the United States. These extremely violent and aggressive street gangs, referred to as sets, have adopted a common gang philosophy. Members use violence to protect and expand their drug distribution. The sets share a comprehensive philosophy, expressed in an oath, a prayer, a song, a motto, a concept of war, and 31 common rules including an Initiation, where a new member must withstand 31 seconds of beating or sexual relations.
    Blood Identifiers:
    o Colors red, black, brown and pink
    o B's up ( ), C's Down ( )
    o MOB = Member of Bloods
    o Dog paws made up of three dots
    o CK Crip Killa
    o 031 / 021
    o Red, black, brown or pink bandanas and wave caps
    o Blatt Blatt
    o Greetings: "What dat red be like?"
    o Referred to each other as dogs
    o DAMU = Brother/Blood
    o DAMUETTE = Sister Bloodettes Ruby Red
    o Blood Love
    o What's popping?
- Crips: Originally from Los Angeles, the Crips are an organization of aggressive and brutal gang members who are heavily involved in the drug

trade. Throughout the 1980's and 1990's the Crips developed intricate networks and a respected reputation with other gangs across America. Crip gangs are well established across the United States.

crips identifiers:
- o Colors blue, gray, orange and purple
- o 6 Pointed Star of David
- o C's up ( ), B's down ( )
- o Blue, gray, orange or purple bandanas or wave caps
- o Crip Walks
- o B's crossed out
- o BK Blood Killa
- o Loc (Love only crips)
- o C-Ya
- o Slobs (Derogatory for Bloods)
- o C's Up Cuzz
- o What's Crackalacking?
- o Refer each other as cousins

- Originally from Chicago, the <u>Latin Kings</u> are extremely violent and a well organized gang. The gang is active in New York, New Jersey and Pennsylvania. Its main source of income is from the distribution of drugs and robbery.

  latin kings identifiers
  - o Colors black and gold
  - o 3 or 5 pointed crowns
  - o Eyebrows cut to form five points
  - o Pittsburgh sports team apparel
  - o Yellow and black bandanas, beads or wave caps

- Originating in Los Angeles, MS 13 is one of most violent street gangs in the United States. Members smuggle and distribute illicit drugs and are extremely violent.

  ms 13 identifiers

- o Heavily tattooed
- o Typical latin gang tattoos
- o "Heavy Metal" tattoos
- o Blue and black bandanas

- The 2005 National Gang Trends Survey completed by gang investigators throughout the nation, revealed Sureno gang members have been identified in over 51% of our nation's cities both big and small.

  (Information courtesy of: NJ office of the Attorney General – Gang Awareness Guide: *Recognize the Signs*)

Gang Signs

"Primo" Sign

"Power"

"Victory"

Number One

Kitchen Crip

Bounty Hunters

Crips: "Cousin"

Bishop

Brims

Athens Park Boys (APBs)

Mafia Crips

H'': Harlem Crip

"C": Crip

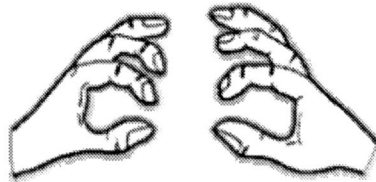

"C-C": Compton Crip

"U": Underground Crip

"E": East

"0": Number Zero

"H": Hoover Crip

Black Stone F--- You

Bloods

Bloods show this to Crip members)

4th Street Brothers

(Information can be found at Gangsta411.com)

NOTES

5 IMPORTANT THINGS I LEARNED FROM THIS SECTION:

1. _____

2. _____

3. _____

4. _____

5. _____

IMMEDIATE ACTION STEPS THAT I WILL TAKE TODAY! :

_____

_____

_____

_____

_____

_____

_____

_____

_____

_____

_____

_____

PERSONAL SAFETY PLAN

What if YOU were attacked / approached? How would YOU respond? You wouldn't go into a sporting game without a plan – so why approach your life / safety that way?

Instructions: Using the information covered in this training handbook – apply what you have learned to develop your personal (family) survival / safety plan:

1. Before starting my day, I will enhance my safety by:

_____
_____
_____

2. In the workplace, I will enhance my safety by:

_____
_____
_____

3. In transition areas (out in public), I will enhance my safety by:

_____
_____
_____

4. In my vehicle, I will enhance my safety by:

_____

_____

_____

5. While traveling, I will enhance my safety by:

_____

_____

_____

6. In my home, I will enhance my safety by:

_____

_____

_____

7. While on the internet, I will enhance my safety by:

_____

_____

_____

** Some things to keep in mind for each area while developing your plan: Escape Route, Safe Place to go to if Attacked, Placement of Fire Extinguishers and First Aid Kits, Placement of Chemical Deterrents, etc.

** **Now that you have taken the time to purchase and read this book and have a plan in place for yourself and your family – UTILIZE IT, MAKE IT A NEW HABIT, MAKE PREVENTION A WAY OF LIFE!**

ORDER FORM

Please send me the follow:

Item:	Quantity:	Price:	Total:
Are Your Habits Killing You? (Book)	_____	$21.95	_____
Alarm Stickers for Windows of Home	_____	$3 / each	_____
Call Police Sign for Back Car Window (Hot Pink)	_____	$6/ each	_____
Key Chain Model of Mace/Pepper Spray	_____	$23.00	_____
Home Model of Mace / Pepper Spray	_____	$26.00	_____

- Tax is included

Shipping and handling
$4.75 per book within the
USA and $8 for Mace _____

Customer Information (please print)
Name: _____

Mailing Address: _____

City: _____ State:_____

Zip: _____

Phone:_____

Fax: _____

Email: _____

Please make check out to: Executive Defense Technology

Credit card: AMEX/ VISA/ MC/ DISCOVER

(Please circle)

Card #

_____ / _____ / _____ / _____

expires: _____

Three digit code on back _____

Signature: _____

ORDERING INFORMATION

Mail order form and payment to:

Executive Defense Technology, LLC

5674 Telegraph Rd #211

St Louis, MO 63129

To contact Executive Defense Technology regarding *"STAYING SAFE IN A DANGEROUS WORLD"* for presentations, lunch and learn brown bag programs, speakers, assemblies, or more extensive "hands on" work with escape techniques please email them at info@execdeftech.com Or for further information visit their website at www.execdeftech.com or www.safetytrainingsystems.net

ORDER FORM

Please send me the follow:

Item: Quantity: Price: Total:

SASSy (Safety and Self-Defense Supplies: for you):

the travel bag contains: _____ $36.00 _____

    mace

    man's tie (it's all about illusion)

    hanging travel wallet for around neck

    personal alarm

    dna/ finger print kit

    wallet card with safety tips

The personal bag contains: _____ $36.00 _____

    fogger mace for hallway if stuck in the home

    mace

    dog bowl

    Rescue Pet Window Cling

    Flash Light

    sign saying house has alarm system

    send police sign for car

    dna/finger print kit

    wallet card with safety tips

               Tax is included

               Shipping and handling

               With in the USA $8 for Mace _____

Customer Information (please print)

Name: _____

Mailing Address: _____

City: _____ State:_____

Zip: _____

Phone:_____

Fax: _____

Email: _____

Please make check out to: Executive Defense Technology

Credit card: AMEX/ VISA/ MC/ DISCOVER

(Please circle)

Card #

_____/_____/_____/_____

expires: _____

Three digit code on back _____

Signature:_____

ORDERING INFORMATION

Mail order form and payment to:

Executive Defense Technology, LLC

5674 Telegraph Rd #211

St Louis, MO 63129 or FAX: 314-894-1148

To contact Executive Defense Technology regarding *"STAYING SAFE IN A DANGEROUS WORLD"* for presentations, lunch and learn brown bag programs, speakers, assemblies, or more extensive "hands on" work with escape techniques please email them at info@execdeftech.com Or for further information visit their website at www.execdeftech.com or www.safetytrainingsystems.net

RESOURCES

Crisis Numbers:

National Center for Missing and Exploited Children 1-800-THE-LOST
(**1-800-843-5678**) A 24-hour, toll-free hotline to report and/or receive sightings of missing and sexually exploited children (www.missingkids.com).

National Runaway Switchboard 1-800-621-4000
A confidential, 24-hour, toll-free hotline that assists runaway and homeless youth in communications with their families and other service providers. The National Runaway Switchboard is supported through a grant from the U.S. Department of Health and Human Services' Family Youth Services Bureau.

Childhelp USA 1-800-4-A-CHILD
A 24-hour, toll-free, confidential hotline offering information about the treatment and prevention of child abuse.

National Victim Center 1-800-FYI-CALL
Provides information referrals and materials free of

charge to victims of violent crime. Distributes safety information and maintains an extensive list of community resources assisting in the battle against victimization.

Girl Power 1-800-729-6686

A public education campaign designed to encourage and empower adolescent girls to make the most of their lives. Many free products are available for girls to use or distribute in their communities (www.health.org/gpower).

Girls Incorporated 1-317-634-7546

Organizes programs in thousands of communities nationwide to educate girls and develop their capacity to be self-sufficient and responsible citizens. Also serves as a vigorous advocate for girls, focusing on their special needs.

National Clearinghouse on Alcohol and Drug Information 1-800-729-6686

TDD 1-800-487-4889 Provides the most current and comprehensive information about substance abuse prevention. They distribute the latest studies, surveys, videocassettes, and materials from government agencies and national substance abuse prevention programs (www.health.org).

National Domestic Violence Hotline: (1-800-799-SAFE) (1-800-799-7233)

Hotline for Elder Abuse and Maltreatment: (Elder Care Locator) (1-800-677-1116)

Hotline for Child Abuse and Maltreatment: 1-800-4-A-CHILD® (1-800-422-4453)

Office of Justice Programs
www.ojp.usdoj.gov

Office of Juvenile Justice and Delinquency Prevention
www.ojjdp.ncjrs.org
1-800-638-8736

Office for Victims of Crime
www.ojp.usdoj.gov/ovc
1-800-627-6872

Drug Enforcement Administration
www.dea.gov

Center for Substance Abuse Treatment (CSAT)
1-800-662-HELP

Community Anti-Drug Coalitions of America
www.CADCA.org

National Clearinghouse for Alcohol and Drug Information (NCADI)
1-800-729-6686
1-877-767-8432 (toll free, in Spanish)
301-468-6433 (fax)
E-mail: info@health.org
www.health.org

National Institute on Drug Abuse
www.clubdrugs.org

Office of National Drug Control Policy Clearinghouse
1-800-666-3332
www.whitehousedrugpolicy.gov

Substance Abuse Treatment Facility Locator
www.findtreatment.samhsa.gov

BIBLIOGRAPHY/ WORKS CITED

"ADASK" Alcoholism and Drug Addiction Statistics, Trends, and Costs. 2004. 30 May 2005 http://www.ni-cor.com/statisticandtrends.html

Addington, L.A., Ruddy, S.A., Miller, A.K., and DeVoe, J.F. (2002). *Are America's Schools Safe? Students Speak Out: 1999 School Crime Supplement* (NCES 2002-331). U.S. Department of Education. Washington, DC: National Center for Education Statistics.

Anderson, M., Kaufman, J., Simon, T., Barrios, L., Paulozzi, L., Ryan, G., Hammond, R., Modzeleski, W., Feucht, T., Potter, L., and the School-Associated Violent Deaths Study Group. (2001). School-Associated Violent Deaths in the United States, 1994-1999. *Journal of the American Medical Association, 286:* 2695-2702.

Aspy, C.B., Oman, R.F., Vesely, S.K., McLeroy, K., Rodine, S., and Marshall, L. (2004). Adolescent Violence: The Protective Effects of Youth Assets. *Journal of Counseling and Development, 82:* 269-277.

Beauvais, F., Chavez, E., Oetting, E., Deffenbacher, J., and Cornell, G. (1996). Drug Use, Violence, and Victimization Among White American, Mexican American, and American Indian Dropouts, Students With Academic Problems, and Students in Good Academic Standing. *Journal of Counseling Psychology, 43:* 292-299.

Beger, R. (2003). The "Worst of Both Worlds": School Security and the Disappearing Fourth Amendment Rights of Students. *Criminal Justice Review, 28:* 336-354.

Brener, N.D., Kann, L., Kinchen, S.A., Grunbaum, J.A., Whalen, L., Eaton, D., Hawkins, J., and Ross, J.G. (2004). Methodology of the Youth Risk Behavior Surveillance System. *Morbidity and Mortality Weekly Report 2004, 53* (No. RR-12): 1-13.

Brener, N.D., Kann, L., and McManus, T. (2003). A Comparison of Two Survey Questions on Race and Ethnicity Among High School Students. *Public Opinion Quarterly, 67:* 227-236.

Cantor, D., and Lynch, J.P. (2000). Self-Report Surveys as Measures of Crime and Criminal Victimization. In D. Duffee (Ed.), *Measurement and Analysis of Crime and Justice* (pp. 85-138). Washington, DC: National Institute of Justice.

Catalano, S.M. (2006). *Criminal Victimization, 2005* (NCJ 214644). U.S. Department of Justice. Washington, DC: Bureau of Justice Statistics.

Centers for Disease Control and Prevention. (2001). Temporal Variations in School-Associated Student Homicide and Suicide Events-United States, 1992-1999. *Morbidity and Mortality Weekly Report, 50*(31): 657-660.

Crick, N.R., and Bigbee, M.A. (1998). Relational and Overt Forms of Peer Victimization: A Multi-informant Crick, N.R., and Bigbee, M.A. (1998). Relational and Overt Forms of Peer Victimization: A Multi-informant Approach. *Journal of Consulting and Clinical Psychology, 66:* 337-347.

Crick, N.R., and Grotpeter, J.K. (1996). Children's Treatment by Peers: Victims of Relational and Overt Aggression. *Development and Psychopathology, 8:* 367-380.

DeBecker, G. (1997). *The gift of fear.* New York, NY: Little, Brown and Company.

Depue, R. (1993). *The avenger personality.* Unpublished manuscript: Academy Group Inc.

DeVoe, J.F., and Kaffenberger, S. (2005). *Student Reports of Bullying: Results From the 2001 School Crime Supplement to the National Crime Victimization Survey* (NCES 2005-310). U.S. Department of Education. Washington, DC: National Center for Education Statistics and Bureau of Justice Statistics.

DeVoe, J.F., Peter, K., Noonan, M., Snyder, T.D., and Baum, K. (2005). *Indicators of School Crime and Safety: 2005* (NCES 2006-001/NCJ 210697). U.S. Departments of Education and Justice. Washington, DC: National Center for Education Statistics.

Eaton, D.K., Kann, L., Kinchen, S., Ross, J., Harris, W.A., Lowry, R., McManus, T., Chyen, D., Shanklin, S., Lim, C., Grunbaum, J.A., Wechsler, H. (2006). Youth Risk Behavior Surveillance-United States, 2005. In *Surveillance Summaries* (MMWR (No. SS-5)). Atlanta, GA: Centers for Disease Control and Prevention.

Elliott, D.S., Hamburg, B.A., and Williams, K.R. (1998). Violence in American Schools: An Overview. In D.S. Elliott, B.A. Hamburg, and K.R. Williams (Eds.), *Violence in American Schools* (pp. 3-18). New York: Cambridge University Press.

Fagan, J., and Wilkinson, D.L. (1998). Social Contexts and Functions of Adolescent Violence. In D.S. Elliott, B.A. Hamburg, and K.R. Williams (Eds.), *Violence in American Schools* (pp. 55-93). New York: Cambridge University Press.

Fairburn, Richard and Col. David Grossman. ***Preparing for School Attacks:*** "The Police Marksman" is published by PoliceOne. Article can be found on line at: http://www.policeone.com/writers/columnists/marksma n/articles/1182387/ Or on Col. Grossman's site at: http://www.killology.com/schoolattack.htm

Federal Bureau of Investigation. Crime in the United States 2000. *Uniform Crime Reports.* Washington, DC: Federal Bureau of Investigation, 2000.

FEMA – Federal Emergency Management Agency; In Depth Guide to Citizen Preparedness

First Estimates from the National Crime Victimization Survey, Identity Theft, 2004 Bureau of Justice Statistics Bulletin

Gang Awareness Guide Provided by the New Jersey Department of Education

Generation Rx? Teens abusing prescriptions .MSNBC.com. Report: More youth getting high on painkillers than on illegal drugs the associated press April 21, 2005. http://www.msnbc.msn.com/id/7582787/print/1/display mode/1098/

Henry, S. (2000). What Is School Violence? An Integrated Definition. *Annals of the American Academy of Political and Social Science, 567:* 16-29.

Highlights from the 46th meeting of the community of Epidemiology Work Group (CEWG) held in Vancouver, British Columbia, Canada on June 8-11, 1999 (discussion on the current epidemiology of drug use)

Javelin Strategy and Research 2006 Identity Fraud Survey Report www.javelinstrategy.com

Jennifer J. Fay and Billie Jo Flerchinger. *Top Secret: Sexual Assault Information For Teenagers Only.* Seattle, Washington: King County Sexual Assault Resource Center, 1988, page 27.

Kachur, S.P., Stennies, G.M., Powell, K.E., Modzeleski, W., Stephens, R., Murphy, R., Kresnow, M., Sleet, D., and Lowry, R. (1996). School-Associated Violent Deaths in the United States, 1992 to 1994. *Journal of the American Medical Association, 275:* 1729- 1733.

Karcher, M. (2002). The Cycle of Violence and Disconnection Among Rural Middle School Students: Teacher Disconnection as a Consequence of Violence. *Journal of School Violence, 1:* 35-51.

Katherine M. Brown, Robert D. Keppel, Joseph G. Weis, and Marvin E. Skeen. *Case Management for Missing Children Homicide Investigation: Executive Summary.* Olympia, Washington: Office of the Attorney General State of Washington and U.S. Department of Justice's Office of Juvenile Justice and Delinquency Prevention, May 2006, page 33. This study is based on the analysis of 735 child-abduction murder cases occurring from 1968 to 2002 in the United States

Kauffman, J., Modzeleski, W., Feucht, T., Simon, T.R., Anderson, M., Shaw, K., Arias, I., and Barrios, L. (2004). School-Associated Suicides-United States, 1994-1999. *Morbidity and Mortality Weekly Report, 53*(22): 476-478.

Laub, J.H., and Lauritsen, J.L. (1998). The Interdependence of School Violence With Neighborhood and Family Conditions. In D.S. Elliott, B.A. Hamburg, and K.R. Williams (Eds.), *Violence in American Schools* (pp. 127-155). New York: Cambridge University Press.

Miller, A. (2003 revised). *Violence in U.S. Public Schools: 2000 School Survey on Crime and Safety* (NCES 2004-314). U.S. Department of Education. Washington, DC: National Center for Education Statistics.

Nansel, T.R., Overpeck, M.D., Haynie, D.L., Ruan, W.J., and Scheidt, P.C. (2003). Relationships Between Bullying and Violence Among U.S. Youth. *Archives of Pediatric and Adolescent Medicine, 157*(4): 348-353.

Nansel, T.R., Overpeck, M., Pilla, R., Ruan, W., Simons-Morton, B., and Scheidt, P. (2001). Bullying Behaviors Among U.S. Youth: Prevalence and Association With Psychosocial Adjustment. *Journal of the American Medical Association, 285:* 2094-2100.

Nolin, M.J., Vaden-Kiernan, N., Feibus, M.L., and Chandler, K.A. (1997). *Student Reports of Availability, Peer Approval, and Use of Alcohol, Marijuana, and Other Drugs at School: 1993* (NCES 97-279). U.S. Department of Education. Washington, DC: National Center for Education Statistics.

Payne, A.A., Gottfredson, D.C., and Gottfredson, G.D. (2003). Schools as Communities: The Relationship Between Communal School Organization, Student Bonding, and School Disorder. *Criminology, 41:* 749-778.

Prinstein, M.J., Boergers, J., and Vernberg, E.M. (2001). Overt and Relational Aggression in Adolescents: Social-Psychological Adjustment of Aggressors and Victims. *Journal of Clinical Child Psychology, 30:* 479-491.

Report published jointly by the National Center for Education Statistics (NCES), Institute of Education Sciences (IES) in the U.S., Department of Education and the Bureau of Justice Statistics (BJS) in the U.S. Department of Justice found on line at: **http://nces.ed.gov/programs/crimeindicators**

Reza, A., Modzeleski, W., Feucht, T., Anderson, M., Simon, T.R., and Barrios, L. (2003). Source of Firearms Used by Students in School-Associated Violent Deaths-United States, 1992-1999. *Morbidity and Mortality Weekly Report, 52*(9): 169-172.

Ringwalt, C.L., Ennett, S., and Johnson, R. (2003). Factors Associated With Fidelity to Substance Use Prevention Curriculum Guides in the Nation's Middle Schools. *Health Education & Behavior, 30:* 375-391.

Scheckner, S., Rollins, S.A., Kaiser-Ulrey, C., and Wagner, R. (2002). School Violence in Children and Adolescents: A Meta-Analysis of Effectiveness. *Journal of School Violence, 1:* 5-34.

Schreck, C.J., and Miller, J.M. (2003). Sources of Fear of Crime at School: What Is the Relative Contribution of Disorder, Individual Characteristics, and School Security? *Journal of School Violence, 2*(4): 57-79.

Small, M., and Dressler-Tetrick, K. (2001). School Violence: An Overview. *Juvenile Justice VIII (I):* 3-12. U.S. Department of Justice. Washington, DC: Office of Justice Programs, Office of Juvenile Justice and Delinquency Prevention.

State of Missouri. Probation and Parole Training Guide.

Stoff, D., Breiling, J. & Maser, J. (1997). *Handbook of antisocial behavior.* New York, NY: Wiley & Sons.

Storch, E.A., Nock, M.K., Masia-Warner, C., and Barlas, M.E. (2003). Peer Victimization and Social-Psychological Adjustment in Hispanic and African-American Children. *Journal of Child & Family Studies, 12:* 439-455.

Strizek, G.A., Pittsonberger, J.L., Riordan, K.E., Lyter, D.M., and Orlofsky, G.F. (2006). *Characteristics of Schools, Districts, Teachers, Principals, and School Libraries in the United States: 2003-04 Schools and Staffing Survey* (NCES 2006-313 Revised). U.S. Department of Education. Washington, DC: National Center for Education Statistics.

"Teen Substance Abuse" GDCADA. 9 March 2005. 28 May 2005 http://www.gdcada.org/statistics/teens.htm

The National Clearinghouse for Alcohol and Drug Information (NCADI). http://www.drugfree.org/portal/DrugIssue/Features/Prescription_MedicineMisuse

Thornton TN, Craft CA, Dahlberg LL, Lynch BS, Baer K. *Best Practices of Youth Violence Prevention: A Sourcebook for Community Action (Rev.).* Atlanta: Centers for Disease Control and Prevention, National Center for Injury Prevention and Control, 2002.

U.S. Department of Education, National Center for Education Statistics. (2004). *Crime and Safety in America's Public Schools: Selected Findings From the School Survey on Crime and Safety* (NCES 2004-370). Washington, DC: U.S. Government Printing Office.

U.S. Department of Education, National Center for Education Statistics. (2003). *Digest of Education Statistics, 2002* (NCES 2003-060). Washington, DC: U.S. Government Printing Office.

U.S. Department of Education, National Center for Education Statistics. (2006). *Digest of Education Statistics, 2005* (NCES 2006-030). Washington, DC: U.S. Government Printing Office.

U.S. Department of Education, National Center for Education Statistics. (forthcoming). *Digest of Education Statistics, 2006* (NCES 2007-017). Washington, DC: U.S. Government Printing Office.

U.S. Department of Justice, Federal Bureau of Investigation. (2006). *Crime in the United States 2005.* Retrieved November 13, 2006, from http://www.fbi.gov/ucr/05cius/data/table_01.html.

Wei, H., and Williams, J.H. (2004). Relationship Between Peer Victimization and School Adjustment in Sixth-Grade Students: Investigating Mediation Effects. *Violence and Victims, 19:* 557-571.